COOKING
SCRAPPY

COOKING SCRAPPY

100 RECIPES TO HELP YOU
Stop Wasting Food,
Save Money,
AND Love What You Eat

Joel Gamoran

HARPER WAVE

HarperCollins books may be purchased for educational, business, or sales promotional use. For information, please e-mail the Special Markets Department at SPsales@harpercollins.com.

FIRST EDITION

Designed by Leah Carlson-Stanisic

Food photography by Jim Henkens

Illustrations by June Park

Library of Congress Cataloging-in-Publication Data

Names: Gamoran, Joel, author.
Title: Cooking scrappy : 100 recipes to help you stop wasting food, save money, and love what you eat / Joel Gamoran.
Description: First edition. | New York, NY : HarperCollins Publishers, [2018] | Includes index.
Identifiers: LCCN 2018020064 | ISBN 9780062862945 (hardcover)
Subjects: LCSH: Cooking (Leftovers) | Food waste. | Food industry and Trade—Waste minimization. | LCGFT: Cookbooks.
Classification: LCC TX652 .G345 2018 | DDC 641.5/52—dc23 LC record available at https://lccn .loc.gov/2018020064

18 19 20 21 22 LSC 10 9 8 7 6 5 4 3 2 1

This book is dedicated to Mom and Dad.
Scraps are simply trash without you.

CONTENTS

FOREWORD

When I was growing up, my mother made sure my siblings and I were dedicated members of the Clean Plate Club. Let's be honest: I am still a tried-and-true member today.

She instilled in us a sense that food was sacred, something to be grateful for; something to savor. My mother taught me that a good meal could be a gathering tool; a prompt for good conversation and companionship. But above all, she taught my brother and sister and me to respect food: to understand where it came from, how it was prepared, and the magical way it somehow nourished both our bodies and hearts.

From the moment I met Joel, I could tell he cared for food with the same warmth and reverence my mother had. He is one of the most enthusiastic and passionate people I've ever met . . . but it's his love for food—and food scraps—that makes Joel one of the most forward-thinking chefs in the business.

That you've picked up this book means you might already be aware of the staggering economic impact of wasted food: 40 percent of the food in the United States is wasted and 20 percent of the food we buy never gets eaten—for the average family of four, that's $1,500 a year in the trash.

But the environmental impact is perhaps even more devastating. Food is the biggest contributor to landfills, and the methane gases that are released contribute more to climate pollution than all the cars in the state of Georgia combined. Our food system is a complicated and global problem, but an alarming 42 percent of our wasted food occurs at home.

That means the at-home chef has a lot of say in this fight against food waste and, frankly, a lot of power to change these statistics.

From the tops of your strawberries to the stalest slices of bread, inside this book you'll find one hundred recipes that will remind you of the power food has to comfort us and nourish us, as well as the power we have to see a little differently, make a few changes, and have a lasting positive impact on the food sources we love.

My mother taught me to respect food, and Joel taught me to save it . . . so I'm inviting you to join a movement that makes real change by getting scrappy. Who's with me?

— Katie Couric

ODUCTION *Why Scrappy?*

So, there I am, freaking out on the F train. Not that that is unusual—it's absolutely normal for me to have massive anxiety on a packed sweaty subway from Manhattan to Brooklyn—but tonight is different. I'm cooking to celebrate my fiancé's new job. I'm an hour and a half late, and there is no way that I am going to beat her home. But, hell, I'm a man in love. I am determined to make this work.

I jet out of the subway, jump on my scooter, and head straight to the butcher to grab one of his rock star racks of lamb. Normally Staubitz Market trims their racks till the bones are bald, but I have plans for the discarded fat-streaked scraps, so I ask for a mess of trim. (Butchers either throw the unsalable stuff they trim from steaks, chops, and roasts into ground meat, or they sell it to a renderer.) *They're usually happy to give it to their good customers.* Back on the scooter, I hop over to the cheap market on Court Street to snag some Yukon Gold potatoes and a handful of dandelion greens. I don't really have a plan. I just figure lamb, potatoes, greens—how can this go wrong?

Crashing through the front door, I barely hit every other step on the way to our third-floor walk-up, completely forgetting that our oven is on the fritz. Also, out of olive oil! Dang, it's too late to go back to the store. I've got just thirty minutes to whip up something spectacular.

I season the lamb with a little cumin, then salt and pepper, and sear the meaty parts in a dry cast-iron skillet. This smells incredible! If you only have one piece of equipment in your kitchen, it's got to be a cast-iron skillet. *The most versatile pan you will ever own!* I move the lamb to one side of the pan and throw in the lamb scraps. In a few minutes, I have a slick of lamb fat for frying the potatoes.

I am making Angiolina's favorite crispy Hasselback potatoes, which call for fanning the taters. No sweat. Got a hack for that. Just put a wooden spoon on a work surface, lay a potato in the hollow of the spoon, and slice. The edges of the spoon stop the knife before it cuts all the way through. Now, normally Hasselbacks are baked, but remember, no oven. No problem. All I need is another pan. I brown the potatoes all over in the lamb fat in the first pan, scatter on salt, pepper, and nutmeg, throw in a fist of water to create some steam, and invert a second pan over the top. *Instant stovetop oven.*

Now all that's left is to sauté the greens and I've made it. Oil!?! What the hell am I going to do for oil? When in doubt, stare into the fridge. And once again the fridge gods deliver. There in the back corner of the top shelf is a single anchovy, slippery in its can of oil. Perfect. Anchovy and oil go into another pan along with some garlic and red chile. Greens in, and I still have ten minutes left before Ang comes home.

I line the kitchen table with some brown parchment paper and scribble "CONGRATS!" down the middle with a marker. I grab some candles left over from Chanukah, melt the bottoms, stick them on a little petri dish, and place them on the table. I don't have speakers, so I stick my phone in a coffee mug to project the sound and click to whatever is first on my playlist as I poke the potatoes to check for tenderness.

The doorknob turns. I give Angiolina a bearhug and let out a huge sigh of relief. We still talk about how good that meal was.

I think about all the meals I've cooked and how the best ones are never overthought and overplanned. They just seem to sort of happen. I'm a trained chef. I've worked in amazing restaurants where I've had access to cutting-edge equipment and stellar ingredients that came together into meals worth hundreds of dollars, but those are not the meals I'm most proud of.

Cooking scrappy celebrates perfection that can be made from the imperfect, the neglected, and the underused. When making the most out of what you have is your only option, you can almost always come up with something gorgeous. Why not cook like this all the time?

Cooking Scrappy

Cooking scrappy is about expanding your mind, the way you cook, and the way you live. A stockpot can be a mixing bowl, but so can the produce drawer from your fridge. Being scrappy is using every resource you have to get from point A to point B. Think outside the recipe box, and be open to using your kitchen, your cooking equipment, *plus the stuff that you never thought to cook on* and all of your ingredients to their absolute max.

I am the National Chef for Sur La Table and I have taught thousands of cooking classes to every level of home cook. In one class I noticed everyone's scrap bowls filled to the brim. I saw shrimp shells, carrot peels, and onion skins. *A bunch of garbage!* Then I took a minute and realized this would never fly in a restaurant. Nothing is allowed to go to waste when you're a restaurant owner. Every cent counts or you will fail.

From the beginning of my cooking career, I knew I didn't want to be locked up in a restaurant kitchen. My professional goal has always been to motivate people to get into their own kitchens and start cooking. I don't think there is a better way to connect with others and with your world. Food waste is a growing concern and is becoming a hot button issue in food news. People are looking for practical ways to curtail their wasteful habits. The following pages are filled with a bazillion ways to get scrappier, better your environmental impact, save money, and eat some life-altering food while you're doing it.

Scrappy Doesn't Mean Crappy

I love creating beautiful food from the ugly and discarded, the typically trashed ingredients that make up almost 50 percent of our nation's landfill. *The United States has more food waste than any other nation on Earth!* It's inspiring to resurrect squeezed-out lemon rinds into a fragrant, flavorful lemon curd that can become the filling for a lemon pie, the base for an Asian lemon sauce, or the centerpiece of a super-sophisticated breakfast of a giant lemon curd pancake (page 43). And unlike lemon curd made solely from the juice, *the typical way of doing it* my curd has the deep, rich aromas of lemon oil that permeates the zest and all the healthy antioxidants that are hidden in the rind.

Just because an ingredient is ugly doesn't mean it's bad. But on the other hand, it doesn't necessarily mean it's good. I never suggest that mistreated ingredients belong in your kitchen. I don't buy produce that has been sprayed and I only support solid sources of meat and seafood, where I know the product was thoughtfully harvested. I cannot promise you that pork fat from a locally raised heritage breed will taste better than fat from a pig raised on a commercial farm, but I truly believe you need to start with great ingredients in order to have amazing scraps.

I want these pages to inspire people to cook scrappy, to think about the hidden potential in everything in their kitchens, but if something is truly unusable, you have to throw it away. If chicken smells off, toss it. If fuzzy mold takes over your raspberries, see ya! This book is about taking the still-vibrant pieces of food that are normally thought of as trash and giving them a second chance. You cannot take something dead and bring it back to life, but you can find delicious uses for ingredients that have been thoughtlessly discarded and transform them into extraordinary food. *That's what scrappy cooking is all about.*

Saves You $$$

If I buy a lobster for $20 and I steam that lobster and eat it, it's a $20 meal. If I take the shells of that same lobster and roast them, cover them with water, and make lobster broth, I can make lobster bisque. One $20 meal now becomes two $10 meals. I can also take the tomalley from inside the lobster's carapace and nudge it into becoming lobster roll. Amend those finances to three meals for $6.67 each—dang cheap for lobster. Cooking scrappy gets the most out of what you buy and allows you to stretch your food dollars to the very brink.

Dozens of dishes in *Cooking Scrappy* illustrate this sort of thrift: there's Shrimp Shell

Chowder (page 73), Aquafaba Ranch and Radishes (page 110), and Fish Collar Cioppino (page 165). There are libations, like Amaretto Peach Stone Sour (page 126) and Vanilla Pod Rum and Coke (page 127), sides of Sweet Corn Cob Grits (page 195), and Strawberry Top Shortcake (page 221) or Spent Coffee Ice Cream (page 215) for dessert. Look for ingredients stamped §. It indicates a scrap from an ingredient that has already been spent. What's leftover is virtually free.

People sometimes confuse transforming the scraps from a previous night's dinner into a new meal as serving leftovers. It's not. Don't get me wrong; I think cooking your leftovers is the soul of being scrappy. The day after Thanksgiving could be the scrappiest day of the year for most Americans. The good ol' Thanksgiving sandwich of leftover turkey, stuffing, and cranberry sauce is tried-and-true scrappiness. Yet it's a mistake to think that this book is about cooking with leftovers. This book is about changing the way you see your ingredients. *Not using up last night's dinner!* Shrimp shells are an inspiring bonus ingredient that you get every time you eat shrimp. The scrappy brain shift is seeing them like that rather than as trash.

If you can change the way you see ingredients, you will begin to ask your fish seller for fish bones or your local farmer for beet tops, and not only will you have amazing ingredients to work with, but also, since there is so little demand for these products, their price will be way more affordable.

Yay, Planet!

Turning your food scraps into meals doesn't just up the quality of your life; it improves the life of the planet. If we are ever going to dial back climate change, reducing food waste has to become a central goal. It is estimated that 20 percent of global warming is caused by food waste. Scraps that end up in landfill, which is what happens whenever you throw food in the trash, are a huge source of methane gas in the atmosphere, a greenhouse gas that is seventy-two times more damaging than carbon dioxide. When you compost your scraps and take care to aerate them, you may reduce methane emissions, but you don't eliminate them. The scrappiest ecological solution to the food waste dilemma is to cook and eat in such a way that nothing gets wasted in the first place. No waste; no problem.

Up Your Cooking Game

Go to the store right now and buy any box of stock you want. Heat it up and pour it in a mug. Do the exact same thing with a stock you make yourself. *There's a scrappy recipe on page 244.* Take a sip of each. If you like the boxed stuff better, send this book back to me and I'll refund whatever you spent on it. Chefs don't just make stock out of the veg and meat scraps left over from prepping menu items in order to save money. They whip up pots of stock because it makes all their dishes taste incredible. Scraps are real fresh ingredients. Any recipe made with them has to be better than its processed packaged counterpart. It takes real stuff to make real food.

The main reason that an ingredient gets tossed is that we don't recognize it as edible. Ever try a carrot top before? If not, you're about to discover a whole new herb that's the abandoned offspring of flat-leaf parsley and arugula. Adopt it into your life and how you cook suddenly takes a turn. Your cooking rut comes unstuck and you can't help but start to make more exciting, better-tasting food. If brown bananas gross you out, you gotta change your mind. That brown color means there are sugars bursting out of the fruit. You will be a better cook, a more dynamic cook, and a more interesting cook the sooner you embrace what you are throwing away.

And if you don't throw out those strawberry tops and vegetable peels, you've got a pantry full of strawberry sauce, strawberry jelly, ice cream, and tea. You've got vegetable pestos, soups, gratins, pasta sauces, and quick breads streaming from your steaming kitchen, simply because you uncovered an undiscovered arsenal for making the most out of "nothing."

A Scrappy Kitchen

My freshman year of college sucked! My parents had just gotten divorced, and I decided to move across the country to go to the University of Connecticut, basically to get as far away from Seattle as possible. I knew absolutely no one. I lived in a tiny dorm room with nothing to cook on, no sink, and no place to put a plate.

One day I had had enough. I was stressed and lonely and decided to do the one thing that actually brought me some peace of mind: cook. I went in search of a kitchen and found one in the basement. It looked like it had never been cleaned. The burners didn't work (shocker!) and the room had zero ventilation. The oven seemed to be okay, though, and I needed a taste of home, bad! I decided to bake my mom's challah.

The gas station down the street unbelievably stocked bread flour and canola oil, and they had a lone packet of yeast that wasn't out of date. Things were looking up. I picked up some eggs from a Dairy Barn on campus and borrowed some honey from a girl down the hall who had a sore throat. I laid out all of my ingredients and realized I needed a bowl to mix everything in. I know! I ran upstairs and grabbed my neighbor's old football helmet. Took out the padding, washed it, and mixed the dough with my hands. I must have counted every minute of the two hours it took for the dough to rise, my hunger for bread and home growing with the dough.

Time to bake. But to bake it right, I needed a baking sheet. I found a piece of scrap metal in the boiler room, scrubbed it, and built my challah right on top. I globbed on some beaten egg for glaze with my fingers, because who had a brush? Then I tossed it in the oven.

Within twenty minutes the entire building

smelled like fresh baked bread. People I had been too freaked out to talk to stopped in to ask what that smell was, and a girl I had a crush on thought it was cute that I was cooking. I will never forget the first bite of bread. It was like being underwater for way too long and sucking in the most amazing breath of fresh air.

Although getting scrappy with ingredients is at the heart of cooking scrappy, employing bruised fruit and veggie trimmings is not the only way to get the most out of what you have. Once you embrace a scrappy attitude, nothing in your kitchen is off limits. Take a set of tongs, for example. Did you know they are a super-powerful citrus squeezer? Ever cut corn and have it end up all over the floor? Use an angel food cake pan: stand the corn on the center post and the pan catches all the kernels as you shave down the cobs. Two deli container lids facing each other become a DIY guide rail for halving a handful of cherry tomatoes in a single slice. And even though your Bolognese has to simmer for hours to reach perfection, where is it written that it has to take up a burner on your stovetop? Anything that can simmer on a stove can simmer just as well, out of the way, in a low oven. At heart, being scrappy requires nothing more than changing your mind. It doesn't call for new equipment or another trip to the corner store. You've got most of what you need right in front of you. All you have to do is start using it.

Building a Scrappier World

Step into a food market in Italy, Japan, or Iceland and you'll notice something different. Fish is sold on the bone. Cauliflower heads are surrounded by a nest of greens. Broccoli has long stems. Chickens have feet, scallops have coral, and yesterday's bread is sold for stuffing and croutons. The parts that we throw away are celebrated all over the world. This can make it a challenge to shop scrappy in the United States, because it means we may have to go hunting to find whole ingredients.

I know your fish seller looks at you cross-eyed when you ask for fish collars, and I hate to have to send you to the Internet to get spent grain from a forward-thinking brewery to make the Spent Grain Graham Crackers on page 235. *Way worth the effort.* But in key ways, cooking scrappy takes us on an adventure together. At the market, in the kitchen, and at the table, we're moving into an uncharted frontier. It's exciting, it's tons of fun, and at times it's going to be challenging.

There's absolutely no law that keeps markets from selling ugly or bruised produce, meat trimmings, or fish bones. The reason that these things aren't available is because food sellers think you're not going to buy them. If we demand it, our food sellers will find those supplies. They're out there. It's just that right now bruised fruit, meat bones, and vegetable trimmings are being thrown out. Remember back in the nineties when organic food was only something that weirdos asked for. Now just about every food company sells organic. We have to create the same demand for food waste.

When I first started cooking scrappy, I was generating all of the scraps from my own cooking, saving up vegetable scraps for soup and stock, blanching and freezing beet greens when I cooked beets, and turning apple cores into apple butter while the apple pie was in the oven, but now I find some of the coolest scrappy ingredients are being generated by the food industry around me. Most food manufacturers still toss their scraps into landfill, but we, you and me, can have a huge effect on food waste by showing businesses that there's a market for products they generate every day but have never thought to sell.

It's as simple as asking your local bakery for stale bread, the produce guy or gal at Whole Foods for the broccoli stalks they hacked off that morning, or the barista on the corner for her spent coffee grounds. Knowing the right questions to ask is powerful. I hope this book arms you when you're at a farmers' market or your local grocery store. And when you find carrot top pesto for sale, or spent grain English muffins, or whey ice pops, buy them. The food world is definitely getting scrappier. All you have to do is open your mind and join in.

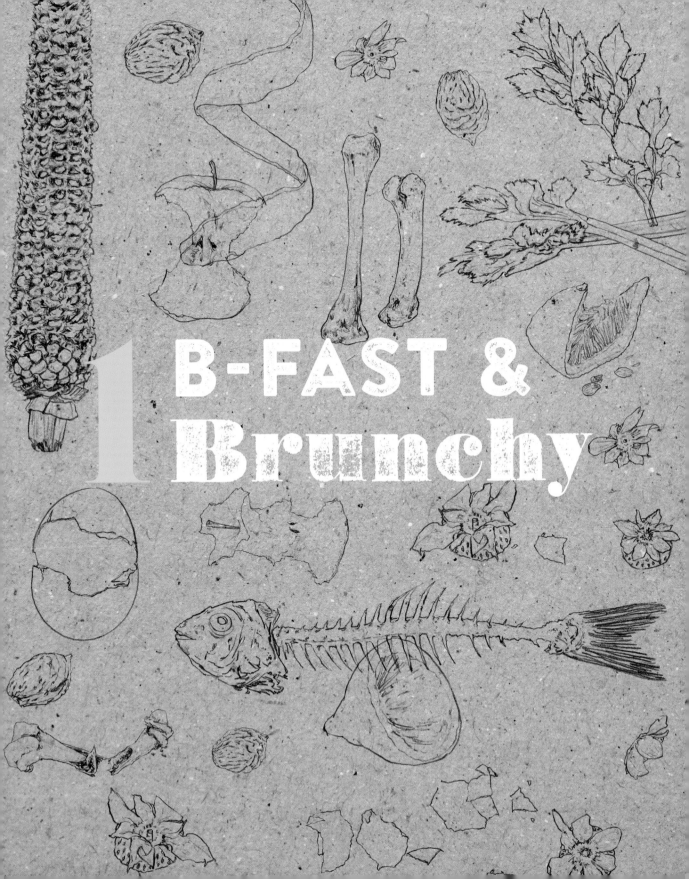

1 B-FAST & Brunchy

Chard
Stems

RAINBOW CHARD STEM SHAKSHUKA (PAGE 20); CHARD STEM
SLAW; SMOKY CHARD STEMS AND BEANS; CHARD STEM GRATIN

LEEK *tops*

LEEK TOP BAKING SHEET HASH (PAGE 30);
LEEK TOP GRATIN; EGGS SCRAMBLED WITH
LEEK TOPS; LEEK TOP PESTO; TOSS IN STOCK

Beet SKIN

SALLY'S BEET SKIN GRAVLAX SANDYS (PAGE 33);
BEET SKIN GRAVLAX (PAGE 35); BEET BORSCHT;
PICKLED EGGS; BEET SKIN PINK SUGAR OR SALT;
BEET BUTTER

Bacon
FAT

BACON FAT BISCUITS AND APPLE BUTTER SANDWICHES (PAGE 36);
SEAFOOD CHOWDER; SCRAMBLED EGGS;
POT PIE CRUST; USE TO BROWN MEAT

Brown *Bananas*

EVERYDAY BROWN BANANA SMOOTHIE (PAGE 45);

OVERRIPE BANANA SHEET CAKE WITH PEANUT BUTTER FROSTING (PAGE 228);

FROZEN BANANA ICE CREAM; BANANA BREAD; BANANA MUFFINS;

BANANA PANCAKES

MANGO PITS.

MANGO PIT JAM MESS (PAGE 46);
MANGO VINEGAR; MANGO SORBET; MANGO DRESSING

Caul *fat*

CAUL FAT MAPLE BREAKFAST SAUSAGE (PAGE 27);
WRAP ROASTED MEATS (INSTEAD OF BACON);
WRAP BURGERS; WRAP MEATLOAF;
RENDER AND FRY YOUR EGGS

TAHINI AUTUMN SQUASH SEED GRANOLA (PAGE 48);
TOASTED PUMPKIN SEEDS; PESTO; MOLE;
ROASTED VEG; BREADS; BRITTLE

Squash
SEEDS

RAINBOW CHARD STEM Shakshuka

Most chard recipes don't use the stems because chard stalks can get fibrous. Rainbow chard stems are insanely sweet and have a stellar crunch. Shakshuka is the perfect spot for them, as they give this rustic one-pan Israeli breakfast a bunch of personality! **SERVES 4**

3 bunches rainbow chard *I know it looks like too much, but it's not . . . really . . . believe me.*

1 fennel bulb, sliced thin, keep the leafy fronds *Celery could be used in place of fennel.*

1 or 2 serrano or jalapeño chiles, sliced

1/2 cup chopped fresh cilantro, stems and all

2 teaspoons ground toasted cumin seeds

2 garlic cloves, sliced

1/4 cup olive oil

Coarse sea salt and fresh ground black pepper

8 large eggs

6 ounces feta cheese, crumbled

Harissa, sriracha, or salsa *as much as you want*

4 to 8 thick slices crusty bread, toasted *for scooping*

Turn the oven to 375°F.

Strip the chard stems from the leaves and cut the stems in 1-inch chunks. Chop the chard leaves into small pieces.

Toss the chard stems, sliced fennel, chiles, cilantro, cumin, garlic, and oil in a large cast-iron skillet, put over medium-high heat, and cook until the vegetables are fairly tender and glistening with aromatic veg juices, about 5 minutes, stirring whenever you want. Add the chopped chard leaves and some S&P and cook for another 5 minutes.

Crack the eggs over the top of the vegetables, season with more S&P, and scatter the cheese over everything. When the oven is up to temp, bake until the egg whites are set but the yolks are still runny, about 8 minutes.

Splotch everything with harissa. Tear up and scatter the fennel fronds all around.

Put it on the table and dive in with a pile of crusty bread.

Leftover Scraps

Egg shells—clarifying stock, deacidifying coffee

Fennel fronds—gremolata, scrambled eggs, salad greens

Feta water—salad dressing, pickling, sauces, soups

Garlic paper—seasoning, stock

Broccoli Rabe AND Sausage Fat FRITTATA

My buddy Snoop from college loves broccoli rabe more than anyone in the world. A long time ago he introduced me to the classic combo of rabe and sausage. The fat that sputters off the sausage makes for the most meat-enriched eggs on the face of the planet. This frittata is cooked low and slow to make it extra creamy. **SERVES 4**

Lots of coarse sea salt

1 bunch broccoli rabe (aka rapini), *stems, leaves, florets—everything* cut into chunks

2 spicy Italian sausages in casing (about 12 ounces), *You can use sweet sausage.* cut in small pieces

2 yellow onions, peeled, halved, and sliced thin

Fresh ground black pepper

6 large eggs

1 cup ricotta cheese *Whipped cream cheese works too.*

2 tablespoons chopped fresh oregano leaves *That's about 6 big sprigs.*

Turn the oven to 325°F.

Boil a lot of salted water in a big pot. *Don't be shy with the salt.* Add the chopped-up broccoli rabe and cook until it is tender, about 3 minutes. Drain it and let it hang while you keep cooking.

Put a medium cast-iron or other ovenproof skillet *something that doesn't have a plastic handle* over medium heat and get it hot. Add the sausage and cook until the fat from the sausage coats the skillet, about 5 minutes. Move the sausage to a medium bowl using a slotted spoon, but leave all that delicious fat in the skillet.

Add the onions to the skillet and cook until softened and starting to brown, about 5 minutes, stirring every now and then. Season with some salt and a few grinds of pepper. Scatter the rabe and sausage evenly over the onions.

Whisk the eggs, ½ cup of the ricotta, the oregano, more salt, and a few more grinds of pepper in the dirty sausage bowl. Pour the egg mixture into the skillet. Use a fork to move the ingredients evenly in the

skillet and cook until the eggs are set across the bottom, about 1 minute.

Put the skillet in the hot oven. Bake until the eggs are puffed and set, about 15 minutes. Cool for about 10 minutes. *Cuts easier if it's not piping hot.* Dot with the rest of the ricotta, cut into wedges, and eat up.

Leftover Scraps

Egg shells—clarifying stock, deacidifying coffee

Onion skins—stock, veg soup, Onion Skin Fried Pickles (page 101)

YESTERDAY'S TORTILLAS Chilaquiles

I used to work the brunch shift with a bunch of ridiculously funny Mexican dishwashers. Every Sunday morning somebody made chilaquiles verdes out of some freeze-burnt or stale tortillas, popping staff meal into the realm of magical eating. This is my version. **SERVES 4**

15 tomatillos, paper removed
Throw it out. Tomatillo paper is trash.

1 onion, peeled and chunked

6 garlic cloves, peeled

1/2 jalapeño chile, chunked, seeds and all

1/2 cup grapeseed oil

12 stale corn tortillas

Coarse sea salt

1 1/2 teaspoons ground cumin

1 small bunch fresh cilantro, stems chopped fine, leaves chopped rough

3 red radishes, tops and all, radishes sliced thin, greens chopped rough

1 tablespoon agave syrup

8 eggs, any size

1 avocado, peeled, pitted, and randomly chunked

2 ounces cotija cheese, crumbled

1 lime, cut into 4 wedges

Turn the oven to 450°F.

Toss the tomatillos, onion, garlic, and chile with 1/4 cup of the oil in a big cast-iron skillet or other ovenproof pan. When the oven is up to temp, bake until the tomatillos are wilted and tender, about 25 minutes.

Tear up the tortillas into bite-size pieces and toss with the remaining oil and some salt on a baking sheet. Bake until crisp, about 10 minutes, tossing halfway through. *Add them in the oven while the tomatillos are cooking if there's room.*

Dump the roasted veggies in a food processor or blender. Add the cumin, chopped cilantro stems, radish greens, agave, and more salt. Blitz until everything is saucy.

Combine this mixture with the toasted tortillas in the cast-iron skillet. Crack the eggs on top and put back in the oven. Bake until the whites of the eggs are set but the yolks are still runny, about 5 minutes.

Top with avocado, sliced radishes, cheese, and cilantro leaves. Serve up with the lime wedges. Dig in.

Leftover Scraps

Onion skins—stock, veg soup, Onion Skin Fried Pickles (page 101)

Garlic paper—seasoning, stock

Egg shells—clarifying stock, deacidifying coffee

Avocado pit and skin—nothin' to be done

Caul Fat MAPLE BREAKFAST SAUSAGE

Just got back from Vermont and every single day there I had maple sausage from a different diner. I love how the salt and sweet flirt. Making sausage from scratch is not my jam. But using sheets of caul fat (available from many online sources) to wrap the patties makes it super easy to bust out my home-made version with tons of flavor. **SERVES 8**

1 pound ground pork

2 tablespoons maple syrup

1/2 whole nutmeg, grated

2 garlic cloves, chopped fine

1/2 teaspoon Aleppo or other red chile flakes

Finely grated zest of 1/2 orange

Leaves from 2 branches rosemary (about 2 tablespoons), chopped fine

1 tablespoon coarse sea salt

1 teaspoon fresh ground black pepper

3 ounces caul fat, cut into 8 pieces

Mix everything except the caul fat in a big bowl.

Scoop the sausage mixture with a 1/4-cup measuring cup into 8 patties. Don't overfill.

Wrap each patty in a piece of caul fat. Do not overlap the caul fat. It's OK if not every inch of sausage is covered.

Put a large cast-iron skillet over medium-low heat. Add the patties. Here's a tip: When cooking a bunch of small pieces, like sausage patties or scallops, it's important to keep track of your timing. Imagine a clock face in your pan, placing the first piece at 12 o'clock, the next at 2, and so on. Flip and test for doneness in that order. Cook until browned on the bottom, about 6 minutes. Flip and cook until cooked through (160°F), about 5 more minutes.

Rest on paper towels for 2 minutes before eating. Don't blot away all the fat. It's delicious.

Leftover Scraps

Orange—juice, marmalade, tea

Rosemary stems—skewering (see page 152), herb butter, herb salt

Rendered fat—fry eggs, potatoes, or anything else.

Schmaltzy POTATO PIE

I'm a hash brown snob. I like them shredded and crispy. These are inspired by my Mom's famous latkes. I'm too impatient to do them in batches, so I just make one giant slab and dig in. **SERVES 6**

3 russet potatoes *Don't peel 'em*

2 spring onions, roots and all, washed and chopped fine

Generous grating of nutmeg

Flaky sea salt, such as Maldon, and fresh ground black pepper

3 tablespoons chicken fat *Schmaltz (page 257)*

Shred the potatoes *coarse* in a food processor or on a box grater. Scrape the shreds onto a flat-weave kitchen towel. Wrap the towel around the potatoes and squeeze out as much moisture as you can into a bowl. The potato juice will be a dark brown color. *Don't worry, it's going bye-bye.* Let it sit for a minute and pour some of the water off. Underneath you'll see a layer of white potato starch *So cool!* Drain the rest of the water, but keep the starch in the bottom of the bowl.

Add the shredded potatoes, all but a small handful of the onions, the nutmeg, and some salt and pepper to the starch *Only use about half the S&P you think it's going to need.* and mix it all up.

Put a large nonstick pan over medium-high heat. Add 2 tablespoons of the chicken fat to the pan. When it melts, add the potatoes. *Don't pack the taters down. You want the steam to dance through the layers.*

Cook until browned at the edges, 10 to 12 minutes. *I usually use a rubber spatula and push down the edges to firm them up.* Cover the pan with a large plate or a cutting board and flip the whole thing over.

Add the remaining tablespoon chicken fat to the pan and gently slide the disk of hash browns back into the pan. If it breaks a little, don't freak. It will solidify back up as it cooks. Cook until browned and crisp on the bottom and cooked through, about another 10 minutes.

Slide out onto a cutting board. Finish with the remaining spring onions. Season with more S&P. *Don't be skimpy.* Let it sit for a minute to let the steam escape. Otherwise the potatoes will be soggy and not as solid. Cut into wedges and eat up.

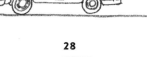

Leek Top BAKING SHEET HASH

Hash is the most common weekend breakfast in my household. Why? Because you can throw anything on a baking sheet, roast it until crispy, plop a few eggs on top, and your Sunday is made. Roasted or sautéed dark green leek tops are just as good and way more beautiful than their more popular white onion sibling—tender, totally flavorful—they're the hero of this hash. **SERVES 4**

1 pound smoked beef brisket or corned beef, *You can go vegetarian by leaving out the meat and goosing up the number of veggies.* cut into bite-size pieces

1 1/2 pounds fingerling potatoes or other small potatoes, cut into small pieces *No need to peel.*

2 red bell peppers, stems and seeds removed, cut into bite-size chunks

3 leeks, *Use it all: roots, whites, light green and dark green leaves.* washed well and sliced thin

4 garlic cloves, chopped fine

1/4 cup grapeseed oil

Coarse sea salt and coarse ground black pepper

8 eggs, any size

1/2 cup dukkah (Egyptian nut and spice mix that you can buy at a fancy market or on the Internet) *Or you can throw on some sesame seeds.*

1 cup chopped fresh herbs, such as parsley, cilantro, and/or mint leaves (if you have some fresh thyme, you can add it, but no more than 1/4 cup *it's a little intense*)

Harissa paste (Moroccan red chile paste), if you want. *You can use Chinese red chile paste.*

Turn the oven to 425°F. Line a rimmed baking sheet with a silicone baking mat or parchment paper.

Toss the brisket, potatoes, bell peppers, leeks, and garlic with the oil on the prepared baking sheet. Season with S&P like you mean it. When the oven is up to temp, bake for 20 minutes, then raise the oven temp to 500°F *to make the edges crisp* and bake for 20 more minutes.

While the vegetables are roasting, boil some water in a large saucepan. Turn the heat down so it simmers and carefully slip in the eggs with a slotted spoon. Simmer for 5 to 5 1/2 minutes.

Get a big bowl of ice water ready. Grab your slotted spoon and move the eggs into the ice water. As soon as the eggs are cool enough to handle, about 30 seconds, crack the shells all over by knocking them against the inside of the bowl. Peel the eggs right in the ice water. *The cold water will help the shells slip right off the egg-so cool!*

Pat the eggs dry and roll them in the dukkah to coat lightly. Cut each egg in half.

Top the hash with the eggs, cut side up. Garnish with the herbs. Serve with harissa, if you want. *You want!*

Leftover Scraps

Red pepper trim—veg stock, any salsa, make rouille

Red onion skins—stock

Mint stems—Mint Stem Sugared Grapefruit (page 44), tea, sub for mint leaves

SALLY'S Beet Skin GRAVLAX SANDYS

In culinary school, I had a job every Saturday morning at the San Francisco Ferry Plaza Farmers Market. I worked for two California hippies, Captain Mike and Sally Heibert. Each morning it was my job to stack slivers of their magical smoked lox on slabs of sourdough, with lots of homemade cream cheese. Here's my tribute to those crisp Bay Area mornings. **SERVES 4**

1 lemon, cut in half

8 ounces whipped cream cheese

2 tablespoons peeled grated fresh horseradish

4 slabs (about 1 inch thick) crusty sourdough bread *For bigger slices, cut the loaf lengthwise.*

12 ounces Beet Skin Gravlax (page 35), sliced thin on a slant

1/4 cup coarsely chopped toasted walnuts

Lavender salt—make it yourself (recipe follows), or purchase it

Squeeze the lemon juice into the cream cheese. Mix in the grated horseradish. Cut the juiced lemon carcass into thin slices.

Spread the bread with cream cheese *As Sally would say, you want to "juice it"!* and top with gravlax, sliced lemon, and walnuts. Sprinkle with lavender salt.

Leftover Scraps

Beet greens/stems—sautéed greens, add to any soup, meat or veg stock

Horseradish peels—soak in vodka or vinegar, juice with tomatoes for a Tomato Seconds Bloody Mary (page 120)

Salmon skin—Salmon Skin Crackers (page 109), fish stock, fry slivers for garnish

Lavender Salt
MAKES 1/2 CUP

2 tablespoons dried lavender

1/2 cup coarse sea salt *I like grey salt.*

Bruise the lavender in a mortar and pestle *Worth it. Don't use a food processor.* Add the salt and mash. Save any extra to season roast chicken, grilled fish, salads, steamed rice; you get the idea.

Beet Skin GRAVLAX

No gravlax will ever compare to Captain Mike and Sally's, but this one's damn close. Beet skin is almost always scrapped, but here it stains the fish and gives it an earthy flavor that I'm addicted to. **SERVES 6**

4 juniper berries, crushed with the side of a knife

¼ cup peeled chopped fresh horseradish root

Zest of 2 Meyer lemons or other lemons

Skin from 2 beets or 1 whole medium red beet, *Root end and stem end included, don't bother trimming.* well scrubbed, cut into chunks

½ cup granulated sugar

¾ cup coarse sea salt

1 pound skin-on wild salmon, pinbones removed *Or ask your fish seller to do this.*

Pulse the juniper berries, horseradish, and lemon zest in a food processor. Add the beet skin (or whole beet) and process until finely chopped. Pulse in the sugar and salt. *Three quick ones should do it.*

Spread half of the mixture into an 8 × 8-inch baking dish and put the salmon on top, skin-side down. *You may need to cut the salmon in half for it to fit in the dish.* Pour the remaining salt mixture on top of the salmon and spread evenly to cover all of the pink meat.

Cover the dish with plastic wrap, pressing it down onto the surface of the salt-caked salmon. Put a weight *A large can of tomatoes works great.* on top of the salmon. Refrigerate for about 48 hours, until the thickest part of the salmon

feels firm when you press on it—it should feel a little bouncy, definitely not hard. *If your salmon fillet is less than ¾ inch thick, check after 24 hours.*

Lift the salmon from the dish and wash all of the beet mixture off the gravlax. Pat dry and set on a cutting board, skin-side down. Cut into paper-thin slices with a long thin-bladed knife. Try to slice on a slant to get wider slices, gliding your knife along the skin at the finish of each slice, like you're a deli dude.

Leftover Scraps

Squeezed lemon—Preserved Squeezed Lemons (page 253), grilled lemon garnish

Horseradish peels—soak in vodka or vinegar, juice with tomatoes for a Tomato Seconds Bloody Mary (page 120)

Bacon Fat BISCUIT AND Apple Butter SANDWICHES

I took my first bite of pork at nineteen while living in Italy. I wasn't quite sure what it was, but I think I saw God. I found out that my epiphany was pancetta (smokeless Italian bacon), and I still can't believe how much I had missed. To ensure this never happens to you, or those you love, make these ridiculously delicious biscuits whenever you've saved enough bacon drippings. **SERVES 8**

8 slices thick-cut bacon

3 cups all-purpose flour, plus more for the board

2 tablespoons granulated sugar

2 ¹/₂ teaspoons baking powder

¹/₂ teaspoon baking soda

³/₄ teaspoon fine sea salt

1 stick (8 tablespoons) cold unsalted butter, cut into small pieces

1 large egg

1 ¹/₄ cups cold buttermilk

Fresh ground black pepper

1 cup apple butter *jarred or Apple Core Butter (page 249)*

Turn the oven to 350°F. Line a rimmed baking sheet with a silicone baking mat.

Lay out the bacon in a single layer on the prepared baking sheet. When the oven is up to temp, bake until crisp, about 20 minutes. Turn off the oven. Lift the bacon onto a few layers of paper towels to blot away the grease and leave the bacon fat in the pan. Stick the pan in the freezer for about 5 minutes to solidify the fat.

Mix the flour, sugar, baking powder, baking soda, and salt in a large bowl. Plop the bacon fat into the dry ingredients in small spoonfuls. Add the butter and, using your fingertips, quickly break up the fat and butter into the dry stuff until it doesn't look dry anymore and the biggest pieces of fat are the size of split peas. *Work fast! You don't want the fat to get too soft.*

Mix the egg and 1 cup of the buttermilk with a fork and pour into the dry ingredients. Mix just enough to make a rough dough. *Better to mix too little than too much.*

Dump out onto a floured board. Pat into a rectangle, fold into thirds like a letter, pat out, and fold into thirds again. Pat into

a 1-inch-thick rectangle, wrap in plastic wrap, and refrigerate until the dough is firm, about 2 hours. *Biscuit dough can sit in the refrigerator for days. Feel free to make this dough up to 3 days ahead.*

Turn the oven to 400°F.

Cut the dough into 8 squares. Brush the tops with the remaining buttermilk and sprinkle with black pepper. When the oven is up to temp, bake until puffed and golden brown, about 30 minutes. Put the biscuits on a cooling rack.

Time to dig in. Cut the cooked bacon slices in half, put them on the baking sheet, and stick it in the oven to warm for a minute. Split the biscuits and sandwich with the apple butter and bacon. Bite; chew; swallow; swoon.

Leftover Scraps
Egg shells—clarifying stock, deacidifying coffee

NAKED Vanilla Pod CUSTARD TOAST

The outer pod of vanilla has just as much flavor as the little black seeds inside, but most people throw it away. I infuse the pods into custards, like this one, and I can tell you, hands down, this is the best French custard toast you will ever eat. **SERVES 4**

6 eggs, any size

2 cups half-and-half

2 saved scraped vanilla pods, cut in small pieces 🔖

¼ cup light brown sugar

1 ½ teaspoons ground nutmeg

1 teaspoon fine sea salt

8 slices (about 1 inch thick) country-style bread (less-than- fresh is best; it soaks up more custard) *You'll need a whole loaf that you can cut yourself to get thick-enough slices.*

4 to 6 tablespoons unsalted butter, plus more for serving

Maple syrup, for serving

Turn the oven to 300°F.

Blitz the eggs, half-and-half, vanilla pods, brown sugar, nutmeg, and salt in a blender until smooth.

Pour half the custard into a rimmed baking sheet. Lay the bread into the custard in a single layer and pour the remaining custard over the top. Turn the slices to make sure they are coated evenly. Do something else for 15 minutes.

A good thing to do while the bread is soaking is to slowly heat a large cast-iron skillet. Start heating on low and gradually increase the heat to medium. This way you'll have an evenly heated skillet when it's time to cook.

When you're ready to cook, add a few tablespoons of the butter to the skillet. As soon as the butter melts, *Don't let it brown,* put a layer of soaked bread in the skillet *Try not to crowd the pan,* and cook until browned, about 3 minutes. Flip and brown on the second side, about 2 minutes. Put the browned toasts on the dirty baking sheet. You don't need to cook the toasts through in the skillet; they're going to finish up in the oven.

Wipe out the skillet and add more butter. Brown the remaining slices in the same way. Once all the toasts are browned and on the baking sheet, put it in the oven, and bake until the toasts spring back when poked, about 10 minutes. Serve right away with more butter and syrup.

Leftover Scraps

Egg shells—clarifying stock, deacidifying coffee

Crushed Blackberry
OLD-FASHIONED DOUGHNUTS *These are gorgeous!*

Seattle summers are the best. Pretty much every street corner is overrun with wild blackberry bushes, so I grew up picking them until I had way too many to deal with = lots of squashed bruised berries at the bottom of the basket. It killed my family to throw these awesome squishy morsels away. We made pancakes, ice cream, jam, and, of course, these stellar doughnuts. **MAKES 12 DOUGHNUTS**

2 1/4 cups cake flour, plus more for the board

1 1/2 teaspoons baking powder

1 teaspoon fine sea salt, plus a little more

1 teaspoon ground nutmeg

1/3 cup light brown sugar

2 tablespoons unsalted butter, softened at room temp

2 egg yolks, any size

1/2 cup sour cream

2 cups bruised or crushed blackberries *but not moldy*

Finely grated zest and juice of 1 lemon *Save the juiced lemon carcasses*

2 cups powdered sugar

Mild-tasting vegetable oil, for frying

Mix the cake flour, baking powder, salt, and nutmeg in a medium bowl.

Beat the brown sugar and butter in the bowl of a stand mixer fitted with a paddle attachment until blended. Add the egg yolks and beat on medium speed until fluffy, about 1 minute. Add the sour cream and beat for 30 seconds more.

Beat in the dry ingredients until just combined. Scrape the dough onto a big sheet of plastic wrap. Pat the dough into a disk and wrap the plastic around it. Refrigerate for 1 hour to firm.

Meanwhile, make the glaze: Combine the berries and half of the lemon juice in a small saucepan. Bring to a boil, then turn down the heat and simmer until thick, about 10 minutes, mashing the berries occasionally with a fork. Stir in the powdered sugar, the remaining lemon juice, and a little salt. Cool.

Remove the dough from the fridge. Dust a work surface with a little flour and pat the dough out into a 1/2-inch-thick rectangle. Cut into 12 squares. *Don't worry if they're not perfect. Rustic is good. You'll get more crispy edges.* Use a twist-off bottle cap to cut a hole in the middle of each doughnut. *I used a wine bottle cap. Save the middles to make doughnut holes.* Use a small sharp knife to score the tops of the doughnuts in the shape of a square around the holes. Transfer the doughnuts to a baking sheet and refrigerate for 30 minutes.

Line a plate with paper towels. Pour about 4 inches of oil into a large heavy-bottomed pot. *It shouldn't come more than one-third of the way up the sides.* Heat over medium heat until a candy or deep-fry thermometer stuck in the oil reads 325°F.

Fry the doughnuts, three or four at a time (depending on

the size of the pot; try not to crowd) score-side up until they float, about 45 seconds. Flip and cook for a minute more, or until browned on that side, then flip again and fry for another minute on the first side. Lift with tongs or a slotted spoon onto the prepared plate to drain.

Dip the cut side of the doughnuts into the glaze. Turn glaze-side up and sprinkle with the lemon zest. Let them hang for about 10 minutes until the glaze sets. *If you can wait that long!*

Leftover Scraps

Squeezed lemons—Preserved Squeezed Lemons (page 253), grilled lemon garnish

Whole Lemon Curd
Giant PANCAKE

Pancakes are my death row food. This one is inspired by my favorite neighborhood joint in Seattle, Talulah's. Instead of a stack, they serve one giant pancake smothered in lemon curd. **SERVES 4**

2 cups cake flour

1 teaspoon baking powder

1/2 teaspoon baking soda

1/2 teaspoon fine sea salt

1/4 cup packed light brown sugar

2 large eggs

2 cups buttermilk

1/2 stick (4 tablespoons) unsalted butter, melted

1/2 cup Whole Lemon Curd (page 250)

Some maple syrup *Because you can't have pancakes without syrup.*

Some more butter *Because more butter is never too much.*

Turn the oven to 400°F.

Mix the flour, baking powder, baking soda, salt, and brown sugar in a large bowl. Mix in the eggs and buttermilk just enough to blend; a few lumps is cool.

When the oven is up to temp, melt the butter in a medium cast-iron skillet over medium-high heat. Stir the melted butter into the batter and pour the batter back into the hot skillet. Toss into the oven and

bake until puffed, browned, and set, about 20 minutes.

Flip onto a serving plate and top with lemon curd, maple syrup, and butter. Dig in. *OMG!*

Leftover Scraps

Egg shells—clarifying stock, deacidifying coffee

Mint Stem SUGARED GRAPEFRUIT

When I was young I would head down to my aunt's in Palm Springs, who'd pick grapefruits off her tree for breakfast, cut them up, and sprinkle them with sugar. Thanks, Aunt Judy. *extravagant breakfast or simple dessert.* **SERVES 4**

2 grapefruits

10 mint sprigs, stems and all, chopped fine

¹/₃ cup demerara sugar or raw sugar

Grate the zest off the grapefruit with a Microplane into a mortar. Throw in the mint and pound until mushy and aromatic. Add the sugar and pound until fine.

Cut the rind from the grapefruit and cut the fruit into thick slices. Arrange the fruit on a plate. Scatter the sugar on top. *It's wet. It's messy. It's frigging delicious.*

Leftover Scraps

Grapefruit peel—Grapefruit Rind Marmalade (page 255)

Everyday **Brown Banana** SMOOTHIE

I drink this smoothie literally every single day. What makes it great is that it uses bananas that are so ripe they're weeping, an indication that their sugar is at maximum sweetness. They're really too soft to eat from the peel, but blended into a smoothie they're the bomb. **SERVES 1**

1 cup almond milk

1 overripe brown banana, peeled, cut into chunks, and frozen

Small handful of ice

2 tablespoons cacao nibs, plus more for topping

2 tablespoons almond butter

Pinch of salt

1 tablespoon honey, plus more for topping

1 teaspoon ground cinnamon, plus more for topping

Put everything *except for the toppings* in a blender. Blitz to mix, about 1 minute. Pour into a glass and top with a few more cacao nibs, a drizzle of honey, and a shake of cinnamon.

Mango Pit JAM MESS

I wish I could say I thought of this first, but my buddy Bijoux told me he used to save mango pits and scrape them naked of all their sweet flesh. Totally inspired me to knock them up into this crazy breakfast dish. **SERVES 4**

½ vanilla bean *pod, seeds, everything*

4 saved mango pits or 2 whole mangoes, peeled and halved

1 cup granulated sugar

1 tablespoon fresh lemon juice

2 cups plain Greek yogurt

1 cup mixed berries (such as strawberries, raspberries, and fresh red currants)

1 tablespoon chia seeds

Split the vanilla bean and scrape out the seeds with a small knife. Save the seeds and scraped pod separately.

Put the mango pits plus any flesh, the sugar, 1 cup water, and the scraped vanilla bean pod in a medium saucepan. Put over high heat, stirring a lot, until everything is bubbling. Then turn it down to as low as you can; cook for about 40 minutes. Every now and then, take tongs and scrape the sides of the pits, releasing as much of the flesh clinging to the pits into the jam as you can. Add a little more water if it starts to brown, but the finished jam should be pretty thick.

Remove the pits and let cool. When cool enough to handle, scrape any flesh still on the pits and stir into the "jam" along with the lemon juice. Throw out the vanilla pod.

In a shallow serving bowl or platter, stir together the vanilla seeds and yogurt. Spread across the bottom. Plop the mango jam on top and gently swirl it through the yogurt. *You want it to look marbled.* Scatter with berries and chia seeds. Dig in!

Leftover Scraps

Squeezed lemon—Preserved Squeezed Lemons (page 253), grilled lemon garnish

Mango skins—dry them and grind them to make amchur powder

TAHINI AUTUMN Squash Seed GRANOLA

The seeds sold as pumpkin seeds don't come from the jack-o-lanterns we think of as pumpkins. In reality, the seeds come from pumpkins that are closer to autumn squashes like acorn, butternut, and delicata. There's no need to ever buy pumpkin seeds, because you get a mess of them every time you cook a squash. **SERVES 4**

1 cup saved squash seeds
1/2 cup plus 1 tablespoon pumpkin seed oil or grapeseed oil
1/4 cup maple syrup
1/4 cup tahini
1/2 cup light brown sugar
3 cups old-fashioned rolled oats
1 teaspoon fine sea salt
1 cup dried cherries (or your favorite dried fruit), chopped rough
Flaky sea salt, such as Maldon

Turn the oven to 300°F.

Line a rimmed baking sheet with a silicone baking mat, parchment paper, or foil.

Toss the squash seeds with 1 tablespoon of the oil right on the lined pan. When the oven is up to temp, bake until dry and just beginning to color, about 10 minutes.

Meanwhile, mix the rest of the oil, the maple syrup, tahini, and brown sugar in a medium bowl. Here's a great hack: Use the same measuring cup and measure the oil first so the maple syrup and tahini slide out of the cup. Mix into the squash seeds directly on the baking sheet with a rubber spatula or big spoon.

In a big mixing bowl, toss the oats and fine sea salt together. Stir in the squash seeds and dump everything back onto the baking sheet. Push into an even layer and bake until toasted, about 40 minutes, turning the baking sheet halfway through. Cool completely and break into bite-size chunks. Stir in the dried cherries and season with some flaky sea salt.

2

Lunch

Pea
Shells

PEA SHELL SOBA NOODLE SALAD (PAGE 61);
FRESH PEA SOUP; PESTO FOR PASTA; SLIVERED IN SALAD;
SPRING RISOTTO; PICKLED PEA SHELLS

Papaya seeds

PAPAYA SEED-DRESSED LITTLE GEMS (PAGE 63);
SUBSTITUTE FOR GREEN PEPPERCORNS;
PICKLED PAPAYA SEEDS

brown AVOCADO

ICED VEG WITH OVERRIPE AVOCADO GODDESS (PAGE 64);
AVOCADO ICE CREAM; AVOCADO BROWNIES;
AVOCADO CHOCOLATE CAKE; CHILLED SOUP

Shrimp
SHELLS

SHRIMP SHELL CHOWDER (PAGE 73);
SCRAPPY LOBSTER ROLL (PAGE 91); SEAFOOD SAUCES;
FISH STOCK; SHRIMP SALT; COMPOUND SEAFOOD BUTTER

Lobster shells

SCRAPPY LOBSTER ROLL (PAGE 91);
SEAFOOD SAUCES; FISH STOCK; SHRIMP SALT;
COMPOUND SEAFOOD BUTTER

Scraped
CORN COBS

CORN COB SOUP (PAGE 77);
VEG STOCK; SWEET TEA; CORN-INFUSED BUTTER FOR POPCORN

Asparagus bottoms

ASPARAGUS END SOUP WITH MINT AND CRISPY POTATO SKINS (PAGE 78);
VEG STOCK; PICKLED SPRING VEG; ASPARAGUS MAYO

Parmesean
RINDS

CHEESE RIND TOMATO BREAD SOUP (PAGE 81);
BEEF SHIN OVEN BOLOGNESE (PAGE 144); ADD TO PASTA WATER;
SIMMER WITH PASTA SAUCE; COOK WITH RISOTTO;
ADD TO BROTH; FRY LIKE HALOUMI

Pea Shell SOBA NOODLE SALAD

Think about it. People love snackin' on peas, shell and all, but when we cook peas, for some reason we treat the shells like trash. Pea shells have incredible pop, are super refreshing, and star in this vibrant salad. **SERVES 4**

7 ounces buckwheat noodles (soba) *about 2 bundles*

1/4 cup tahini

2 tablespoons Vietnamese fish sauce (nam pla)

2 tablespoons light brown sugar

Finely grated zest and juice of 2 limes

Fresh pea shells from English peas, or whole snap peas, sliced thin *You want about 2 cups of sliced pea shells, but the amount isn't crucial.*

2 small watermelon radishes (or other red radish), sliced thin

1/2 to 1 small Fresno or serrano chile, sliced thin *your heat, your choice*

1 handful fresh cilantro, leaves chopped rough, stems chopped fine *Don't over-chop your herb leaves. They brown insanely fast.*

1 handful fresh mint leaves, chopped rough

Black sesame seeds, for garnish

Boil a big pot of water. This is one time not to salt the water. We'll be adding lots of salty fish sauce later. Add the noodles and cook until tender, about 3 minutes. Drain into a strainer and rinse with a lot of cool water. Shake it out.

Mix the tahini, fish sauce, brown sugar, and lime zest and juice in a large bowl. Toss in the cooked noodles, pea shells, radishes, chile, and herbs. If it looks dry, add a little water a few tablespoons at a time. Sprinkle with black sesame seeds and go for it.

Leftover Scraps

Mint stems—Mint Stem Sugared Grapefruit (page 44), tea, sub for mint leaves

Squeezed lime—pickled lime, grilled garnish

Papaya Seed-Dressed LITTLE GEMS

A while ago my brother won a contest at work and took me to Hawaii. We found a rad little farm that grew awesome gigantic guavas and papayas. For breakfast, the farmer would dish up these plump papaya halves with the seeds still in them. I fell in love with the pop and pepperiness of the seeds and vowed to never throw them away again. **SERVES 4, PLUS EXTRA DRESSING**

1 small papaya *It's OK if it's not super ripe.*

1 tablespoon Dijon mustard

Finely grated zest and chopped juicy flesh of 1 lime *Trim the white pith and save it for scrap.*

1 1/2 teaspoons honey

1 teaspoon fish sauce

Fine sea salt

1/3 cup vegetable oil or any mild-tasting oil

5 ounces Little Gem lettuce *You can substitute any butter or Bibb lettuce.*

2 shallots, peeled and sliced thin

1/3 cup roasted peanuts, chopped rough

Small handful of fresh mint leaves

1/2 to 1 small Fresno or serrano chile, sliced thin *The heat is up to you.*

Cut the papaya in half. Scrape out the seeds into a blender.

Peel the green skin from the papaya and toss it. *So sad! Papaya skin is a completely useless scrap.* With the same vegetable peeler, plane three quarters of the peeled papaya flesh into ribbons (you'll get about 3 cups of papaya ribbons) and put in a large bowl. *Easiest to do this on the outside where the fruit is firmer.* Cut the remaining quarter of the papaya into chunks and throw into the blender with the seeds.

Add the mustard, lime zest and flesh, honey, fish sauce, and salt. Blitz until smooth. With the machine on low, take the thingy out of the center of the lid and stream in the oil through the top to make a smooth, thick dressing.

Toss the lettuce, shallots, peanuts, mint, and chile with the papaya strips. Drizzle with enough dressing to coat. Don't drown it. *You'll have some left over.*

Leftover Scraps

Extra dressing—green salads, marinades

Mint stems—Mint Stem Sugared Grapefruit (page 44), tea, sub for mint leaves

Lime pith—pickled lime, tea

ICED VEG WITH Overripe Avocado GODDESS

When you bring an avocado into your home, you immediately start the clock ticking on a timeline toward perfect and ripe, which can easily slide into mushy and brown if you don't pay attention. Just-ripe avocados flirt with being creamy, but when they move a little past prime into their soft stage, they explode with richness. And you get to wallow in it when you whip up this incredible dip. **SERVES 4 TO 6**

1 overripe avocado *dark skin, soft but not bruised*

Finely grated zest and juice of 1 lemon

1 cup plain Greek yogurt

1/4 cup mayonnaise

1 bunch radishes, with tops

Handful of fresh basil *stems and all*

Handful of fresh mint leaves

1/4 cup chopped fresh chives

2 tablespoons white wine vinegar

1 tablespoon honey

2 garlic cloves

Coarse sea salt and fresh ground black pepper

1 quart assorted uncooked vegetables (such as halved cherry tomatoes, strips of bell peppers, cucumber sticks, slant-cut carrots, endive leaves, sliced fennel, celery sticks, snap peas)

Cut the avocado in half lengthwise, running the knife around the pit. Jam the knife into the pit and pop it out. Squeeze the soft avocado flesh from the halves into a food processor. Add the lemon zest and juice, the yogurt, mayonnaise, 2 radish tops, the basil, mint, chives, vinegar, honey, garlic, and S&P to taste and blitz until smooth. *If you make this in a blender, it will be really thick.*

Scrape into a nice-looking bowl and put on a big platter surrounded by radishes and assorted raw vegetables for dunking.

Leftover Scraps

Mint stems—Mint Stem Sugared Grapefruit (page 44), tea, sub for mint leaves

Radish tops—salad greens, pesto, sub for watercress

Avocado pit and skin—nothin' to be done

Squeezed lemons—Preserved Squeezed Lemons (page 253), grilled lemon garnish

CHICORIES CAESAR WITH Anchovy Oil CROUTONS

Caesar salad has been my absolute favorite forever, mostly due to my deep love of great croutons. I like a crouton I can sink my teeth into. These are kissed with anchovy. *Amazing!* **SERVES 4**

1 (1-inch-thick) slice rustic bread, cut into 1-inch cubes

1 (2-ounce) tin anchovies in olive oil

Coarse sea salt and fresh ground black pepper

1 tablespoon Dijon mustard

2 garlic cloves

1/2 teaspoon honey

1 1/2 cups shredded Parmesan cheese

Juice of 2 lemons *Helpful Hack: Juice through a slotted spoon to catch the seeds*

2 green onions, roots, dark greens, everything, sliced

1/4 cup grapeseed oil

1 small head radicchio, halved, cored, and cut into bite-size chunks

1 head escarole, broken into leaves, washed, dried, and sliced thin

Turn the oven to 425°F.

Toss the bread cubes with the oil from the can of anchovies *Just open the anchovy can halfway to help you hold back the anchovies when you pour out the oil.* on a baking sheet or an ovenproof skillet. Season with a little S&P. When the oven is up to temp, bake until browned and crispy on the outside but still soft inside, about 10 minutes. *Catch the anchovy oil tip (page 147)*

To make the dressing, blitz 4 anchovies (about half the can), the mustard, garlic, honey, 1/2 cup of the Parm, the lemon juice, root ends and dark green ends of the green onions, 1/2 teaspoon salt, and more

pepper until smooth. Take the thingy out of the center of the lid and with the blender running, drizzle the grapeseed oil through the hole. Blend until creamy.

Toss the remaining green onion centers with the radicchio and escarole. Add the dressing and toss until everything is coated. Add the rest of the shredded Parm and the croutons and toss; not too much. Eat.

Leftover Scraps

Anchovies—pasta sauce, pizza topping, salad dressing

Squeezed lemons—Preserved Squeezed Lemons (page 253), grilled lemon garnish

Stale Bread PANZANELLA

My buddy Ben Whitten and I rented a car when we were nineteen and got lost in the Tuscan country-side. We must have eaten our weight in panzanella (all different types) as we waddled through the hills. The one thing all the varieties embraced was yesterday's stale bread. It taught me the beauty of stale. Stale bread isn't bad fresh bread. It's stellar dried bread, ready to soak up a mess of fragrant tomato pulp, pungent garlic, and fruity cold-pressed olive oil. **SERVES 4**

2 yellow bell peppers

3 tablespoons extra-virgin olive oil

Fine or coarse sea salt

8 ounces stale crusty bread, torn into bite-size pieces (about 5 cups)

1 pint cherry or grape tomatoes, halved *Cool hack for halving cherry tomatoes on next page.*

2 Persian or Kirby cucumbers, halved lengthwise, sliced thin

Handful of fresh basil (leaves and stems), torn

2 garlic cloves, chopped fine

2 tablespoons white balsamic vinegar

Fresh ground black pepper

1 tablespoon dried oregano

Turn the oven to 425°F.

Put the bell peppers in an ovenproof skillet or pie pan. Drizzle with 1 tablespoon of the oil and a little salt. When the oven is up to temp, roast the peppers until browned, about 30 minutes. Remove from the oven and cover with an overturned bowl. Let them hang out to steam and soften for about 20 minutes.

Peel off the skin, tear the bell peppers open with your fingers, remove the cores and seeds, and cut or tear the flesh into small pieces. Put the pieces in a large bowl; save the accumulated juices. *Seeds are end-of-the-line scraps. Chuck 'em—there's nothing you can do with them.*

Put the torn bread in the pepper skillet. Season with salt and massage with any remaining pepper drippings. *Really scrunch it!* Bake until golden, 10 to 15 minutes. Cool enough to touch.

Scrunch the tomatoes a little and throw them in with the peppers along with the toasted bread, cucumbers, basil, garlic, vinegar, the rest of the oil, more salt, and as much pepper as you like. Mix well. Sprinkle with the oregano and toss. *You want to see some of the oregano on top.* Taste and season with more S&P if you want. Let everything hang out for about 10 minutes to mellow before serving.

Leftover Scraps

Roasted pepper skin—add charred flavor to soups, chilis, stews

Garlic paper—seasoning, stock

Cherry Tomato Hack: You'll need 2 deli container lids. Put one right side up on a work surface. Put cherry or grape tomatoes, as many as will fit, on the lid. Put the other lid upside down over the tomatoes, so the raised rims of the two lids match up. With one hand, put gentle pressure on the surface of the top lid. Slide the blade of a sharp knife horizontally into the space between the two lids on one side and run it through till it comes out the other side. Lift the top lid and you've got a mess of halved tomatoes.

Wilted Lettuce Soup

Most people store lettuce all wrong, making lots of wet rag lettuce heads—droopy and wilty, like depressed weeping willows. Guess what? Wilted lettuce has its own thing going on. It's still refreshing, and it can add a ton to lots of different dishes. I love it in this spring-inspired soup. No one will ever know your secret ingredient came from the back of the fridge. **SERVES 6**

2 tablespoons unsalted butter

1 medium onion, peeled and sliced thin

2 garlic cloves, sliced thin

Coarse sea salt and fresh ground black pepper

1 medium turnip, end trimmed, scrubbed, and diced *Leave the peel on.*

1 large Yukon Gold potato, scrubbed and diced *Again, no peeling.*

1 quart vegetable stock *homemade (page 245) or bought*

4 cups wilted and/or fresh lettuce leaves, any type

1 cup frozen peas

Juice of 1/2 lemon

1 cup plain yogurt, for garnish

Aleppo chile flakes or other red chile flakes, for garnish

Melt the butter in a medium saucepan over medium heat. Add the onion and garlic and season with 1/2 teaspoon salt. Cook until the onion stops looking raw, about 3 minutes.

Add the turnip, potato, and vegetable stock and simmer for 20 minutes. Remove from the heat, add the lettuce leaves and peas, and stir until the lettuce leaves are very soft.

Puree the soup in a blender until silky smooth. Stir in the lemon juice and season with more S&P. *Amount depends on the saltiness of your stock.*

Serve each bowl swirled with yogurt and topped with Aleppo chile flakes.

Leftover Scraps

Squeezed lemon—Preserved Squeezed Lemons (page 253), grilled lemon garnish

Turnip ends—beef or vegetable soup, add to mashed potatoes, any stew, any meat or veg stock

Egg shells—clarifying stock, deacidifying coffee

Garlic paper—seasoning, stock

TOMATO AND NECTARINE SALAD
WITH Cucumber Seed DRESSING

Most of the time recipes for cucumber salad call for removing the seeds so they don't water down the dressing. Here they are the dressing, and the results are awesome, creamy, and lush. **SERVES 4**

1 garlic clove, peeled

1 whole unpeeled cucumber (on the small side), seeds scooped out and saved

1 slice bread, crusts removed, cut up

1/2 teaspoon honey

1 tablespoon champagne vinegar *or other white wine vinegar*

2 tablespoons extra-virgin olive oil

Coarse sea salt

2 tomatoes

2 nectarines, pitted

6 fresh basil leaves, plus a few more little ones for garnish

Pinch of red chile flakes

Blitz the garlic clove, cucumber seeds, bread, honey, and vinegar in a blender. Turn the blender on to medium-high. Take the thingy out of the center of the lid and drizzle the oil through the hole. Blend on high speed until creamy. Season with 1/2 teaspoon salt.

Cut up the tomatoes, nectarines, and cucumber into random slabs and toss in a bowl. Tear in the basil and add the dressing. Toss and sprinkle with more salt and the chile flakes. Garnish with baby basil leaves.

Leftover Scraps

Bread crust—breadcrumbs, croutons

Nectarine pits—soak in liquor, infuse in custard

Basil stems—herb salt, pesto, pasta sauce

Garlic paper—seasoning, stock

Shrimp Shell CHOWDER

Shrimp shells were the first thing to make me scrappy. When I was in culinary school we used them to give a seafood hint to fish stock. That was cool, but then I found you can grind them and get even more flavor, and they're completely edible; you don't need to strain them out. My mind was totally blown.

SERVES 8

1 pound (26–30) shrimp, peeled, shells saved

2 ears corn on the cob, kernels removed (see below), naked cobs saved

1 onion, peel and top saved, chopped fine

1 small celery root (about 12 ounces), scrubbed and peeled, peel saved, cut into small pieces

1 fennel bulb, brown sections and hard stalks removed and saved, some fronds saved, cut into small pieces

2 thick strips bacon, cut into small pieces

2 Yukon Gold potatoes, cut into 1/4-inch cubes

4 garlic cloves, chopped fine

Coarse sea salt and fresh ground black pepper

Put the shrimp shells, naked corn cobs, onion peel and top, celery root peel, and fennel trimmings in a large saucepan or small stockpot. Cover with water (about 2 quarts total) and simmer until flavorful, 45 minutes to 1 hour. Strain.

Cook the bacon in a heavy soup pot over medium heat until the bacon pieces just start to brown and the bottom of the pot is coated with bacon fat. Add the chopped onion, celery root, fennel, and potato, cover, and cook until the veggies lose their raw look, stirring every now and then, about 5 minutes. Stir in the garlic and corn kernels and cook for another minute.

Pour the shrimp stock through a fine strainer into the soup pot. Simmer until the vegetables are tender, about 10 minutes.

Ladle half of the veggies with some of the liquid into a blender and blitz into a rough puree. *Start slow. The soup is hot and you don't want to blow off the lid.* Return to the soup pot. Or use a stick blender and blend right in the soup pot until you get the consistency you like.

Chop the shrimp into bite-size pieces. Get the soup simmering; stir in the shrimp, turn off the heat, and wait 5 minutes. Season with S&P and garnish with chopped fennel fronds.

Hack to Remove Corn Kernels from a Cob: Stick the cob upright in the center hole of a tube pan. Slide a knife down the cob, cutting off the corn kernels into the pan.

Leftover Scraps

Garlic paper—seasoning, stock

Spent Coffee Short Rib CHILI

Imagine how many cups of coffee are brewed every single morning, and every one of those cups results in a couple of tablespoons of used coffee grounds. The aroma of coffee is intoxicating, and it's still there even after the beans are spent. I love their roasted chocolate notes with assertive red meats, like the short ribs in this chili. **SERVES 6**

1 tablespoon grapeseed oil

2 ½ pounds boneless beef short ribs

Coarse sea salt

3 medium yellow onions, peeled and chopped

2 tablespoons chili powder

2 tablespoons ground cumin

1 tablespoon smoked paprika

2 tablespoons dark brown sugar

1 star anise

½ cup brandy

1 (28-ounce) can diced tomatoes

2 tablespoons spent coffee grounds *$*

1 quart chicken stock, homemade (page 244) or bought

1 ½ cups French brown lentils

1 cup packaged fried shallots
Get them at any Asian grocery or online, if you want

2 cups shredded sharp white cheddar cheese, if you want

Get the oil hot in a large Dutch oven over medium-high heat. Season the short ribs with a good amount of salt. Brown the meat on all sides for about 3 minutes per side. Don't crowd the pot. If the pieces of meat touch, they will steam and not brown. Remove them and continue browning the rest of the short ribs. *Remove onto the pot lid, turned upside down to catch the juices.*

Add the onions to the Dutch oven and cook until they start to brown, about 5 minutes. Stir when it looks like they could use stirring.

Stir in the ground spices, brown sugar, and star anise and cook until the smell of the spices is strong, a minute or so.

Add the brandy. Stand back, as the brandy could flame. If it does, cover with a lid to douse the flames. *Another lid, not the one holding the short ribs.* Cook until the pot is almost dry. Add the tomatoes with their juices. Add the spent coffee grounds, stock, short ribs, and any accumulated juices. Cover and simmer over low heat until the meat is fork-tender, about 2½ hours.

Stir in the lentils and continue to simmer, covered, until the lentils are tender, about 30 minutes.

Remove the short ribs from the chili. Using two forks, shred the meat into bite-size pieces. Stir back into the chili.

Serve garnished with the fried shallots and cheese.

Leftover Scraps

Onion skin—stock, veg soup, Onion Skin Fried Pickles (page 101)

Corn Cob SOUP

This is a perfect example of how scraps can up your cooking game. Why would you put any stock in a corn soup other than corn stock? Be sure you're holding on to something when you eat this soup. It's hard to keep your balance when your eyes are rolling back in your head. **SERVES 8**

8 ears of corn

1 stick (4 tablespoons) unsalted butter

Coarse sea salt

1/4 cup vegetable oil

Handful of fresh sage leaves

Aleppo or other red chile flakes, for garnish, if you want

Remove the kernels from the cobs (see page 73). Now you want to "milk" the stripped cobs. Hold the cobs upright on a plate and run the back of a knife down the length of the bare-naked cobs, shaving the juices from them. *It's called "corn milk."*

Put the "milked" cobs in a large pot, cover with about 2 quarts of water, and boil for 20 minutes. *This is a quick stock. You want to keep it boiling.*

Use tongs to remove the cobs. Keep the stock warm.

Melt the butter in a large Dutch oven or soup pot. Set aside about 2 cups corn and add the rest to the pot. Season with salt and cook until bright yellow and tender, about 10 minutes, stirring whenever you get the urge.

Dump the cooked corn in a blender. Add 1 1/2 cups of the cob stock. Blitz until completely smooth. *Be careful blending hot liquid, it can splash.* When done it should look like thin pancake batter. Add more stock if you need to.

Add the corn puree back to the pot. Add the saved corn kernels and corn milk and cook over low heat until the kernels

cook through, about 5 minutes. Add more stock if the soup is too thick. Keep warm.

Add the oil to a medium skillet over medium-high heat. Add the sage leaves and fry until crisp and the oil stops bubbling. *You might need to tip the skillet to create a pool of oil deep enough to cover the leaves.* Transfer to paper towels to drain.

Ladle the soup into bowls. Top with the fried sage, chile flakes, and a drizzle of the sage-infused frying oil.

Leftover Scraps

Corn stock—freeze and use in other soups, chowder, or risotto

Sage stems—herb salt, stuffing, gravy

Asparagus End SOUP WITH MINT AND Crispy Potato Skins

Have you ever had asparagus strands caught in your teeth? It means they weren't completely trimmed. Most recipes call for throwing the stringy bottoms away, but I'm here to tell you, you don't have to. Blitz them and you get all their flavor without a speck of stringy fiber. **SERVES 4**

2 tablespoons extra-virgin olive oil, plus more for finishing

1 large yellow onion, peeled and chopped small

3 garlic cloves, chopped rough

Fine sea salt

Bottoms from 2 bunches asparagus or 1 bunch whole asparagus, cut into 1-inch lengths *Chopping the asparagus ends makes them blitz evenly.*

¼ cup dry sherry, plus more for finishing

1 cup frozen peas

2 handfuls fresh mint leaves

Aleppo or other red chile flakes

Spicy Potato Skin Crisps (page 113), recommended, but not a have-to

Put the oil in a medium saucepan or soup pot over medium heat. Add the onion and garlic and a pinch of salt. Cover and cook until tender, about 5 minutes. *Covering a pot gets everything steamy and cooking fast.*

Throw in your asparagus, cover, and cook for another 2 to 3 minutes. Pour in the sherry and boil for a few seconds. Add 2 cups water, cover, reduce the heat, and simmer until the asparagus is fork-tender, 20 minutes or so.

Add the peas and cook for a minute, no longer. *You don't want to overcook the peas or they will lose their color.* Take the pot off the heat and throw in the mint.

Blitz the soup in a blender until smooth. Keep the top vent open to release steam, but cover with a dish towel to keep stuff from splashing out. Season with more salt and another swig of sherry.

Serve in bowls, swirl with oil, sprinkle on some chile flakes, and drop a few spicy potato skin crisps on top to blow everybody's asparagus soup assumptions.

Leftover Scraps

Onion skin—stock, veg soup, Onion Skin Fried Pickles (page 101)

Garlic paper—seasoning, stock

Mint stems—Mint Stem Sugared Grapefruit (page 44), tea, sub for mint leaves

Cheese Rind TOMATO BREAD SOUP

When studying in Italy I learned that Parmesan rind had as much value as the shaved cheese itself. You want everyone to flip over your recipes? Throw in a Parm rind. **SERVES 4**

2 tablespoons extra-virgin olive oil, plus more for finishing

1 onion, peeled and chopped

1/2 Fresno or serrano chile, stem and about half the seeds removed, chopped fine

5 garlic cloves, chopped fine

4 pounds (7 or 8) tomatoes, *Good use for seconds!* bite-size chopped, plus the stems, if you have them

A hunk of Parmesan rind, the bigger the better

Coarse sea salt

1 cup (about 1 slice) chopped-up stale rustic bread, the size of small croutons

4 basil leaves (don't trim the stems)

Aleppo or other red chile flakes

Put the oil in a large saucepan over medium-low heat. Stir in the onion and chile, cover, and cook until tender, about 3 minutes. Add the garlic and cook for another 30 seconds.

Stir in the tomatoes. Drop in the tomato stems if you have any and the Parmesan rind. Season with salt. Cook, covered, until everything is soft, about 40 minutes.

Take out the tomato stems and cheese rind and discard. *They've done their job.* Stir in the bread and keep stirring until all the pieces are wet. Blend half the soup and stir back into the chunky half to give it a little creaminess. Adjust the thickness with a little water, if you think it needs it.

Top with torn-up basil, a good glug of oil, and a big pinch of chile flakes.

Leftover Scraps

Chile seeds—toast for seasoning

Onion skin—stock, veg soup, Onion Skin Fried Pickles (page 101)

Garlic paper—seasoning, stock

CSALT (Chicken Skin, AVOCADO, LETTUCE, AND TOMATO) SANDWICH

Everyone thinks they love the smell of roast chicken, but really everyone loves the smell of roast chicken skin. Many people strip the best part of the chicken off the meat before its roasted. It's just what you need to make this jaw-dropping killer of a sandwich. **SERVES 1**

2 sheets of chicken breast skin or 4 sheets of chicken thigh skin

2 tablespoons mayonnaise

2 thin slices rustic bread

Coarse sea salt

3 slices tomato

3 slices avocado

2 red leaf lettuce leaves

Hot pepper sauce

Turn the oven to 450°F. Line a rimmed baking sheet with a silicone baking mat or parchment paper.

Lay the chicken skin in a single layer on the prepared baking sheet. Place another rimmed baking sheet of the same size on top right-side up so that the top pan sits right on top of the chicken skin to keep it from puffing up. When the oven is up to temp, bake until crisp, about 25 minutes.

Five minutes before the chicken skin is supposed to be done, spread 1 1/2 teaspoons of the mayonnaise on one side of each slice of bread. Put mayo-side up on the top baking sheet in the oven to toast.

When the chicken skin is browned and crispy, take the top sheet off. Remove the bottom sheet from the oven and put the sheet of toast back in. Let the chicken skin cool to firm up, about 2 minutes, before you assemble the sandwich. Keep the rendered chicken fat that's in the pan.

Take the toast out of the oven and spread the remaining mayo on the bare sides of the slices of bread. Top one slice with the chicken skin, *Fold the skin if you need to, to make it fit on the bread.* a sprinkling of salt, the tomato slices, avocado slices, more salt, the lettuce leaves, and a squirt of hot pepper sauce. Top with the remaining slice of bread mayo-spread side down. Cut in half and chomp away.

Leftover Scraps

Rendered chicken fat—frying potatoes, or anything else

Avocado pit and skin—nothin' to be done

Lamb Neck NAAN'WICH

In San Francisco, after a late shift on the line, I would head down to my favorite Indian place and get a midnight naan'wich—day-old naan wrapped around leftover curry. It was cheap, satisfying, and, to this day, one of my favorite sandwiches. This one takes advantage of lamb neck, a cut that's not often sold 'cause it grosses folks out. All I've got to say is they're missing out. **SERVES 4**

1/4 cup grapeseed oil, plus more if needed

4 pounds bone-in lamb neck, cut into 3-inch-thick cross-sections

Coarse sea salt

1 small bunch fresh cilantro, stems chopped fine, leaves whole

1 medium yellow onion, peeled and chopped small

8 garlic cloves, chopped fine

3 tablespoons curry powder *Use your favorite.*

3 medium tomatoes, *Use seconds.* chopped up

1 tablespoon honey

2 large shallots, peeled and sliced thin

1 lime, zest grated fine, fruit cut into wedges

4 pieces naan bread

Plain Greek yogurt, for serving

Aleppo or other chile flakes, for serving

Chermoula sauce (from Feta Water Farro, page 88), if you want

Put the oil in a large Dutch oven over medium-high heat. Season the lamb with salt and add just enough pieces to the pot so that they fill the bottom without crowding. *You'll probably need to do this in 2 or 3 batches.* Sear the lamb pieces all over until nicely browned, about 3 minutes per side. Remove and continue with the rest of the lamb. *Use the overturned pot lid to rest the browned lamb. It catches the juices and you don't have to clean another plate.*

Turn the heat down to medium. Add the cilantro stems, onion, and garlic. Cook until the onion is tender, about 5 minutes, scraping the bottom of the pot to incorporate any browned bits of lamb. *Add a little more oil if the pan seems dry.*

Add the curry powder and cook until your kitchen smells fragrant, maybe a couple of seconds. Stir in the tomatoes and honey. *Use your hands to squeeze the tomatoes over the pot before throwing them in.*

Add 2 cups water. *No need to mess with stock here. Water does the job and lets the flavor of the lamb shine through.* When the pot's bubbling, add the browned lamb and any accumulated juices. Turn the heat down to low, cover, and simmer until the lamb is fall-off-the-bone tender, 2 to 2 1/2 hours.

Cool for a bit so that you can use your fingers to pull the meat off the bones. Sort through the meat for any tiny bones. *Use the overturned pot lid again to sort the meat.* Return the lamb meat to the pot and stir into any pan juices.

Right on your cutting board, mix the shallots, cilantro leaves, and lime zest.

Warm the naan in a dry cast-iron skillet for a few minutes on each side. Put each piece of naan on a plate. Slather with yogurt, pile on the lamb and shallot salad, and sprinkle with Aleppo chile flakes. For extra credit, drizzle with chermoula.

Leftover Scraps

Lamb bones—stock

Garlic and shallot skins—seasoning, stock

Onion skin—stock, veg soup, Onion Skin Fried Pickles (page 101)

Cilantro roots—stock, salsa

Shriveled Grape CHICKEN SALAD

Ever buy grapes and forget about them? Me too. Embrace these shriveled sweet-tart morsels and turn them into homemade raisins. This chicken salad recipe is my wife's go-to. It rocks! **SERVES 4**

1 cup green grapes (also works with red), shriveled or otherwise

1 whole roasted chicken, with skin

3 tablespoons mayonnaise

2 teaspoon Dijon mustard

1 tablespoon white wine vinegar

Coarse sea salt and fresh ground black pepper

3 ribs celery with leaves, sliced thin

1 tablespoon chopped fresh dill

Turn the oven to 200°F.

Scatter the grapes on a rimmed baking sheet and bake until shrunken and shriveled, about 6 hours. *If you've got the oven space you can dry cherry tomatoes, sliced onions, or garlic cloves at the same time.*

Separate the chicken skin from the meat. Shred the chicken meat. Put the skin on a baking sheet in a single layer and cook under the broiler until browned, about 3 minutes. Rest for 3 minutes to cool and crisp. Tear the skin into bite-size pieces.

Mix the mayo, mustard, and vinegar in a serving bowl. Season with S&P. Add the celery, chicken meat, chopped dill, and shriveled grapes. Toss to coat everything with dressing.

Top with the chicken skin and dish up.

Feta Water FARRO

Next time you buy feta you'll notice it's floating in a bucket of water—water that inevitably gets poured down the drain. Take a sip; it's briny, for sure, but a little tangy too. It actually packs a punch. I like to cook grains in it for a little extra oomph. **SERVES 4**

Farro

Extra-virgin olive oil

1 medium yellow onion, peeled and chopped small

4 garlic cloves, chopped fine

1 cup whole farro

3/4 cup feta brine, plus 4 ounces feta cheese for topping

1 bunch carrots with tops (1 to 1 1/2 pounds), scrubbed and cut into 1-inch pieces *Cut on a slant. Chop the tops up and add to chermoula.*

1 teaspoon ground cumin

Coarse sea salt

Chermoula

2 garlic cloves

1 teaspoon ground coriander

1 teaspoon ground cumin

1 teaspoon smoked paprika

1 small bunch fresh cilantro, leaves and stems, chopped *Cut the stems smaller than the leaves—they're fibrous.*

1 small bunch fresh Italian (flat-leaf) parsley, leaves and stems, chopped

Large handful of fresh mint leaves

Reserved carrot tops from Farro

Finely grated zest and juice of 1 lemon

1 cup extra-virgin olive oil

Coarse sea salt

Harissa paste mixed with a little water, if you want

Turn the oven to 425°F. Heat 1 tablespoon oil in a medium saucepan over medium heat. Add the onion and cook for a few minutes, until softened. Add the garlic and cook for another minute. Add the farro and cook, stirring once in a while, until it smells toasty, about 3 minutes.

Add the feta brine and 1 cup water and bring to a boil. Cover, turn down the heat, and simmer until the farro is tender and most of the liquid is gone, about 25 minutes. Remove the lid and simmer for another 5 minutes to get rid of any remaining water. Keep warm.

While the farro is cooking, toss the carrots (*save the tops for later*) with 1 tablespoon oil, the cumin, and 1/2 teaspoon salt in a large ovenproof skillet. *I like cast-iron. You get great color.* When the oven is up to temp, roast until browned and a bit charred, about 30 minutes. Let cool.

To make the the chermoula, put the garlic, spices, herbs, carrot tops, and lemon zest and juice in a food processor. *Better than a blender, texture is more rustic.* Blitz until chopped fine, scraping down the sides to keep everything moving. Scrape into a bowl and stir in the oil. Season with salt.

Helpful Hack: To get onion and/or garlic stink off your hands, rub them with parsley stems.

Stir 2 heaping spoonfuls of chermoula into the warm farro. Mix in the carrots. Put on a platter and top with the feta and a little more chermoula and some harissa, if you want.

Leftover Scraps

Mint stems—Mint Stem Sugared Grapefruit (page 44), tea, sub for mint leaves

Onion skin—stock, veg soup, Onion Skin Fried Pickles (page 101)

Garlic paper—seasoning, stock

SCRAPPY Lobster Roll

I'm not the kind of lobster guy who goes for big tender chunks drenched in drawn butter. I'm more the kind who likes to see how much I can get out of my ingredients. So, one day, after Ang and I had a spectacular lobster dinner, I had the idea to take last night's lobster shells and infuse them into the leftover butter. Lobster shell butter? Yeah, it's a thing. **SERVES 4**

3 live lobsters, about 1 ¼ pounds each

1 tablespoon tomato paste

2 sticks (16 tablespoons) unsalted butter (Note: you'll have some extra butter)

1 lemon, zest finely grated, fruit cut into wedges

4 New England–style split-top hot dog buns

1 bunch fresh chives, chopped fine

Coarse sea salt and fresh ground black pepper

Big handful of stale or fresh potato ships *If you want— you want.*

Put 2 inches of water in a large stockpot over high heat. When it boils, add the lobsters, cover, and cook until bright red, about 10 minutes. Lift the lobsters out of the pot with tongs and cool until they're cool enough to grab, about 20 minutes. *Save the lobster water as a simple seafood stock.*

Crack the shells with a lobster cracker or a hammer. Dig out the meat from the tails and the claws and cut any big pieces into 1-inch chunks. You can refrigerate the lobster if you want, or keep it warm if you're making the rolls right away.

Put a large pot over high heat. *Use the same pot you used to cook the lobsters.* Add the lobster shells and tomato paste and cook for a few minutes, until aromatic, stirring most of the time. Stir the butter in until it melts and coats the shells. When the butter starts to foam, turn off the heat, add the lemon zest, and let it hang out to take on some flavor from the zest, about 10 minutes. Pour the butter off the shells.

Heat a large skillet over medium heat. Lightly brush a little lobster butter on each side of each hot dog bun. Put the buns in the skillet and toast for a couple minutes on each side.

Add the chives and 4 tablespoons of the butter to the lobster meat. Season with salt and pepper. Stuff into the rolls and squeeze the lemon over top. Crush the chips in your hands and sprinkle onto each sandwich. Start eating. *What a gorgeous sandwich!*

Leftover Scraps

Extra lobster butter—use in seafood risotto, bisques, pasta

Lobster water—use for stock

3 Bites & APPS

Onion
Skins

ONION SKIN FRIED PICKLES (PAGE 101);
ENRICH COLOR OF STOCK; SEASONING FOR COMPOUND BUTTER;
ONION SALT

FISH *skeleton*

INDIAN SPICED FRIED FISH BONES (PAGE 102);

FISH STOCK (DUH! PAGE 243);

COMPOUND SEAFOOD BUTTER

Potato *skins*

SPICY POTATO SKIN CRISPS (PAGE 113);
FRY 'EM AND TOSS IN SALADS; ADD TO STUFFING;
UM-M-M, PIZZA TOPPING WITH BLUE CHEESE AND ONIONS;
HASH WITH ONIONS AND EGGS.

Lardo CORNBREAD WITH *Hot Pepper Honey* LARDO BUTTER

Lardo is cured fat. Fat is yummy. You can't use it too much. Great butchers and Italian specialty shops carry lardo all the time, and any butcher can get it for you. Just ask. **SERVES 8**

2 ounces lardo

1 stick (8 tablespoons) unsalted butter

1/2 cup sugar

1/2 cup honey

2 large eggs

1 cup buttermilk

1 cup fine yellow cornmeal

1 cup all-purpose flour

1 teaspoon fine sea salt

1/2 teaspoon baking soda

1 teaspoon medium hot sauce, such as sriracha

Turn the oven to 400ºF.

Cook the lardo and half of the butter in a medium cast-iron skillet over medium heat until half of the fat has rendered from the lardo and the butter is just beginning to color, about 5 minutes. Fish out the solid pieces of lardo and put them on a plate.

Beat the sugar, 1/4 cup of the honey, the eggs, and the buttermilk in a large bowl. Stir in the cornmeal, flour, 1/2 teaspoon of the salt, and the baking soda. Pour in the melted lardo and butter.

Heat the cast-iron skillet *Don't wipe or wash out the grease in* *the skillet* over high heat until smoking. Pour in the batter and slip the skillet into the hot oven. Bake until puffed and browned and a tester stuck in the center comes out with a crumb clinging to it, about 20 minutes.

While the cornbread is baking, put the solid pieces of lardo, the rest of the butter, rest of the honey, rest of the salt, and the hot sauce in a food processor. Blitz until smooth. This could take a while. If there are a few specks of lardo still visible, that's fine.

Cool the cornbread for 10 minutes. Cut into wedges and serve with the whipped lardo butter. *Unbelievable!*

Leftover Scraps

Egg shells—uclarifying stock, deacidifying coffee

Onion Skin FRIED PICKLES

I had already thrown away more onion skins than Kleenex when I found out they were edible. I just about lost it. Ground into batter, they take any fried food, especially fried pickles, to another planet.

SERVES 4

Any mild-tasting vegetable oil, for frying

¹/₂ cup onion skins and ends

1 ¹/₂ cups all-purpose flour

1 teaspoon salt

¹/₂ teaspoon fresh ground black pepper

1 ¹/₂ cups lager beer *flat or fizzy*

Couple shakes of hot pepper sauce

2 cups dill pickle slices, drained

1 cup Aquafaba Ranch (page 110), for dipping

Heat 4 inches of oil in a heavy saucepan over medium heat to 375°F.

Blitz the onion skins, 1 cup of the flour, the salt, pepper, beer, and hot sauce in a high-speed blender into a smooth batter.

Pat the pickle slices with paper towels until dry and dredge in the remaining flour. Pat off excess flour and dunk in the batter. Lift with tongs and drop into the hot oil. Fry, a few at a time, until golden brown, about 3 minutes.

Using a slotted spoon, put the fried pickles on paper towels to drain. Serve hot, with aquafaba ranch for dipping. *Tart tangy pickles and rich fatty fry! What could be better?*

Leftover Scraps

Pickle juice—Pickle Jartini (page 128), Pickle Juice–Brined Pork Chops (page 160), marinades, pickling brine

Fried Fish Bones

If there's any ingredient that epitomizes garbage, it's fish carcass. Think cartoon cats prowling an alley strewn with trash, stink squiggles floating overhead. In reality, fish bones are a crispy snack waiting to happen. Lots of cultures eat bones. When fried, small bones become so crunchy they're more like chips than fish. You gotta get on the train. **SERVES 2**

Any mild-tasting vegetable oil, for frying

2 small white-fleshed fish skeletons, no heads *I like branzino.*

Lots of coarse sea salt

2 teaspoons of your favorite curry spice mix

Lemon wedges, if you want

Heat 4 inches of oil in a heavy saucepan over medium heat to 400°F.

Drop in the skeletons and fry until browned and crispy, about 4 minutes. *The crispier you get them, the more tender they will be.*

Remove with a slotted spoon to a sheet of newspaper or some paper towels for draining. Season with lots of salt and the curry spice mix. Squirt with lemon and get chomping. Wash down with beer.

Squished Tomato TOAST

You will find *pan con tomate* everywhere in Spain—fine restaurants, roadside stands, bars. Made from squishy, overripe, bursting-at-the-seams tomatoes, all you do is rub the cut fruit hard against crunchy toasts, like you're using a giant eraser, until the surface of the bread gets soaked with tomato goo. When a tomato isn't pretty on the outside, its very ugliness is a sign of all the juicy beauty waiting to burst out. **SERVES 4**

4 slabs (1-inch-thick) crusty sourdough or country bread

¼ cup extra-virgin olive oil

Coarse sea salt and fresh ground black pepper

1 large garlic clove, skin on, end trimmed *This will make it easier to rub later.*

1 very ripe soft tomato, cut in half crosswise *The riper, the better.*

4 ounces paper-thin-sliced Iberico ham or prosciutto, if you want

Set up a grill for medium-high heat, or put a cast-iron grill *ridged* pan over medium-high heat.

Drizzle both sides of the bread with the oil and season with salt and pepper. Place on the grill and weigh down with a heavy pot. *A skillet weighed down with a big can of tomatoes works great.* Grill for 2 to 3 minutes, until charred. Flip the toast, weigh down again, and continue to grill on the second side for another 2 minutes. Remove from the heat.

Rub the bread with the garlic clove. Rub the toasts with the cut sides of the tomato (like you're using a blackboard eraser), so that the flesh of the tomato is worked into the surface of the toasts. Only the tomato skin and a thin layer of tomato flesh should be left. *Every ugly duckling is a swan.* Top with the ham (if using). Start chomping!

Leftover Scraps

Garlic ends—minced garlic, seasoning, stock

Tomato skins—stock, salsa, pasta

Green Tomato JAM, CHEESE, AND CRACKERS

What's up with green tomatoes? It seems like the only way people eat them is fried. Their tart, sweet, lemony personality is too often overlooked. Green (unripe) tomatoes have something that a red ripe tomato can never bring. Stop bypassing the green ones. They're gorgeous! **MAKES ABOUT 1¹/₂ CUPS JAM (ABOUT 12 SERVINGS)**

1 ¹/₂ pounds green *underripe* tomatoes, chopped (about 4 ¹/₂ cups)

1 cup granulated sugar

1 teaspoon ground coriander

¹/₂ teaspoon salt

Your favorite cheddar cheese
I like Beecher's Flagship.

Your favorite crackers
I like Carr's Whole Wheat.

Aleppo or other hot chile flakes, for serving

Simmer the tomatoes, sugar, coriander, and salt in a medium pot over medium-low heat until thick, about 1 hour, stirring every once in a while. Cool to room temp before digging in. You can store in a tightly closed container in the refrigerator for about a month.

To eat: Put some cheese on a cracker and top with a spoonful of jam and a few specks of chile flakes. *So easy! So delish!*

Salmon Skin CRACKERS

I've taught thousands of people to cook fish. Most of them throw out the skin. I never understood that. The skin, especially from rich fatty fish like salmon, becomes extra-crunchy when roasted, a way to fry it without extra fat. Down these crispy "crackers" as a snack with a cold beer. They are awesome spread with whitefish salad, salmon rillettes, or crushed over a green salad. **SERVES 4**

2 teaspoons vegetable oil

Skin from 1 side of salmon
Make sure it's scraped clean of scales. Your fish seller will do this.

1 teaspoon soy sauce

1 tablespoon sesame seeds

¼ teaspoon Aleppo or other red chile flakes

1 teaspoon garlic powder

Turn the oven to 275°F.

You're going to need 2 flat (no rims) baking sheets. Cover one with foil. Drizzle half the oil on the foil. Spread the salmon skin flat on the oiled foil. *You may need to cut the skin in half so that it fits on the foil.* Rub the skin with the rest of the oil and the soy sauce. Top with the sesame seeds, chile flakes, and garlic powder. Cover with another sheet of foil and the other baking sheet. *This will keep the skin from curling up as it bakes.*

When the oven is up to temp, bake until dry, about 1 hour. Remove the top sheet and foil and bake for another 30 minutes, or until crispy. Cool completely before breaking into pieces.

Aquafaba RANCH AND RADISHES

I know it sounds trashy, but I've loved ranch dressing ever since I was a little boy, even though the cream did a number on my tummy. This version, made from the drained liquid from canned chickpeas, is lighter, zippier, and a lot healthier than traditional ranch. Great for your vegan buddies. **SERVES ABOUT 6**

¹/₄ cup aquafaba *the liquid from canned chickpeas* 💲

1 tablespoon apple cider vinegar

1 garlic clove, chopped fine

¹/₂ teaspoon granulated sugar

¹/₂ teaspoon ground brown mustard seeds

³/₄ teaspoon fine sea salt

³/₄ cup vegetable oil

1 tablespoon chopped fresh chives

Finely grated zest and juice of ¹/₂ lemon

1 teaspoon onion powder

¹/₂ teaspoon dried oregano

¹/₄ teaspoon fresh ground black pepper

1 big bunch radishes (with tops), cut in half if large, for dipping

Blitz the aquafaba, vinegar, garlic, sugar, mustard seeds, and salt using a stick blender or upright blender on low speed. Drizzle in the oil while blending until thickened. Stir in the chives, lemon zest and juice, onion powder, oregano, and pepper. *I like to stir these in so the herbs don't get ground up and turn everything green.*

Throw the radishes and their tops on a serving plate and drizzle with some of the dip. *Serve the rest in a bowl for actual dipping.*

Leftover Scraps

Squeezed lemon—Preserved Squeezed Lemons (page 253), grilled lemon garnish

SPICY Potato Skin CRISPS

I came up with these late one night when all I had was some frozen potato peels saved from past meals. I needed something crispy, crunchy, salty, and naughty. The thin skins fry up extra-crispy. I could inhale them by the bowlful, and I have. **SERVES 4**

1 ounce Parmesan cheese, grated (about ⅓ cup)

1 teaspoon onion powder

1 teaspoon garlic powder

½ teaspoon chili powder

½ teaspoon smoked paprika

½ teaspoon ground turmeric

This is more for color than flavor.

Peels from 8 washed Yukon Gold potatoes 💲

2 teaspoons vegetable oil

Turn the oven to 400°F.

Stir the Parm, onion, garlic, and chili powders, the paprika, and turmeric in a small bowl. Toss about ¼ cup of this cheese mixture with the potato peels and oil on a rimmed baking sheet. Drag into an even layer *with your fingers* that pretty much covers the pan.

Bake until crispy, about 25 minutes. Sprinkle with a little more spice mix. *Store the extra spice mix in the fridge and use to sprinkle on popcorn or roasted vegetables. It'll keep for about a month.*

The crisps are best eaten immediately. *These don't store well.*

Scrappy
HOUR

4

Tomato
seconds

TOMATO SECONDS BLOODY MARY (PAGE 120);
MARINARA SAUCE; GAZPACHO; SALSA;
TOMATO TOASTS

PEACH PITS

AMARETTO PEACH STONE SOUR (PAGE 126);
PEACH VODKA; PEACH SYRUP;
FLAVORING ICE CREAM OR CUSTARD

Apple *skin*

APPLE SKIN HARD SPARKLING CIDER (PAGE 125);
INFUSED SPIRITS; APPLE SKIN CRISPS; APPLE SKIN
APPLESAUCE; FLAVORED SYRUPS

Pineapple
RIND

PINEAPPLE RIND TIKI COCKTAIL (PAGE 131);
PINEAPPLE CORE FOSTER (PAGE 217); SCRAPPY WATER (PAGE 256);
FLAVOR SIMPLE SYRUP; PINEAPPLE CARAMEL

Tomato Seconds BLOODY MARY

Raid every farm stand you know for their tomato seconds and rock out with this Bloody Mary. **SERVES 4**

6 over-the-hill tomatoes (about 2 1/2 pounds), bruises and all, moldy parts cut out

A big handful of celery leaves 💲

A couple of onion ends 💲

1 cup beef stock or water

1 teaspoon sea salt

1/2 teaspoon fresh ground black pepper

1/4 cup fresh lime juice

1/3 cup prepared white horseradish

3 tablespoons Worcestershire sauce

1 cup vodka

4 ribs celery, for garnish

4 lime wedges, for garnish

Chop the tomatoes, celery leaves, and onion ends coarsely and put them in a big saucepan with the stock, salt, and pepper. Cook over medium heat until everything is very soft, about 15 minutes. Cool to room temp.

Add the lime juice, horseradish, and Worcestershire sauce and blitz in a blender or with a stick blender. Pour through a strainer to take out any big pieces of onion and tomato skin. You'll have about 4 cups. Chill.

To whip up a cocktail, mix 1 cup of the tomato base and 1/4 cup of the vodka in a tall glass filled with ice. Garnish with a celery rib and a lime wedge.

Leftover Scraps

Squeezed limes—Pickled lime, grilled garnish

Sumo Peel NEGRONI

Hands down, Negroni is my drink of destiny. Soaking sumo peels in your Campari plays a citrus chord that makes this diva sing. **SERVES 8**

Peels from 2 or 3 Sumo mandarin oranges (depending on size), chopped fine §

1 cup Campari

1 cup red (sweet) vermouth

2 cups gin

1 teaspoon orange bitters

8 strips Sumo mandarin orange zest

Put the Sumo mandarin peel in a jar with the Campari and vermouth, seal the lid, and let it hang out for a few days (2 to 3). Taste for orange flavor and let it hang longer if you want more. Strain out the peel.

For each Negroni, put 2 tablespoons of the sumo-infused booze with $\frac{1}{4}$ cup gin and 2 shakes of bitters in a shaker filled with ice. Shake like heck until the shaker is so cold you're having a hard time keeping hold of it. Strain into a chilled cocktail glass garnished with a ribbon of Sumo zest.

Apple Skin HARD *Sparkling* CIDER

So many desserts call for peeling apples. Save those peels. Apple skins are slightly tannic and deliver a caramel quality that enriches this hard cider. Gulp it freezing cold anytime or sip it warm when the weather turns wintry. **SERVES 6**

Peels, cores, stems, and seeds from 6 apples
1 3/4 cups vodka
3 cups lager beer
1 1/2 cups seltzer

Fill a quart jar with the apple scraps. Add the vodka and push down on the apple stuff so that all of it is submerged in the vodka. Screw on the cap and put it out of the way until the vodka is flavored with apple, about 3 days. Strain the liquid and throw away the solids. *They have done their duty.*

To whip up the "cider," mix the apple vodka and beer. It can be stored in the refrigerator if you don't want to drink it right away. When you are ready to drink, pour about 3/4 cup in a tall glass over lots of ice. Add about 1/4 cup seltzer to each glass, stir, and get busy.

AMARETTO Peach Stone SOUR

Do you like almonds? Save your peach stones and make this perfect sipping liqueur that comes to life when mixed with a tart splash of citrus. **SERVES 4**

4 to 6 peach pits *The more pits you use the less time you will need to flavor the booze.*

1 cup amaretto

1/2 cup orange juice

1/4 cup fresh lemon juice

8 dashes of Angostura bitters

Put the peach pits in a jar with the amaretto, seal the lid, and let it hang out for a few days (2 to 3). Taste for peachiness and let it hang longer if you want more fruit flavor. Remove the pits and discard. *They've done what they can do.*

For each cocktail, shake 1/4 cup peach pit amaretto, 2 tablespoons orange juice, and 1 tablespoon lemon juice with ice until the shaker is painfully frosty. Strain into a chilled cocktail glass. Drip 2 drops of bitters on top and swirl with a toothpick. Salute.

Leftover Scraps

Squeezed lemon—Preserved Squeezed Lemons (page 253), grilled lemon garnish

Vanilla Pod
RUM AND COKE

All I have to say . . . this drink is so good and so damn easy you feel like you're cheating. **SERVE 4**

2 scraped vanilla pods,
chopped up 💲

1 cup light or golden rum

2 cups Coca-Cola

4 lime wedges

Put the chopped-up vanilla pods in a jar with the rum, seal the lid, and let it hang out for about a week. Taste for strength and let it hang longer if you want more vanilla flavor. Remove the pods and reserve the rum.

To turn it into a cocktail, pour 1/4 cup of vanilla rum into a tall glass filled with ice. Add 1/2 cup Coke and stir a few strokes. Squeeze in the lime and drop in the wedge. Start sipping.

Pickle JARTINI

My cousins Steven and Stan Feinberg taught me to break the fast on Yom Kippur with a shot of vodka and a chaser of pickle juice. This drink's an ode to them and the Jewish New Year. **SERVES 1**

Pinch of brown mustard seeds, crushed with the side of a knife

2 teaspoons pickle brine

1 1/2 teaspoons dry white vermouth

1/3 cup vodka

1 strip tomato skin, rolled and toothpicked
It'll look like a rosebud.

Rub the mustard seeds all over the inside of a cocktail glass. Brush out the loose seeds. It's fine if a few cling to the glass.

Shake the pickle brine, vermouth, and vodka with ice. *Not too much.* Put a cube in the glass and pour the jartini over the top. Sit the tomato rose on the cube and take a photo. Drink.

Pineapple Rind TIKI COCKTAIL

This stuff is dangerous. Keep out of reach of humans. It goes down too easy. **SERVES 4**

Rind and core from 1 medium pineapple, chopped coarse 💲

1 1/3 cups golden rum

2 cups pineapple juice

1/2 cup orange juice

1/2 cup coconut milk (light is probably rich enough)

4 pineapple wedges, roasted over a high fire, if you want *Stick a skewer in the wedge and hold over a high burner, like you're toasting marshmallows, until charred on the edges.*

Fill a quart jar with the chopped pineapple scraps. You will need to pack it down to get everything to fit. Add the rum, which should completely cover the fruit. Screw on the lid and put it out of the way to flavor, about 3 days.

Drain the liquid through a strainer into a measuring cup. You'll have about 1 1/3 cups.

For each cocktail, mix 1/3 cup pineapple peel–flavored rum, 1/2 cup pineapple juice, 2 tablespoons orange juice, and 2 tablespoons coconut milk in a shaker filled with ice. Shake until frosty, about 30 seconds. Pour into a chilled glass loaded with plenty of crushed ice and garnish with a wedge of roasted pineapple.

5
Dinner

Rosemary
stems

ROSEMARY STEM GRILLED LAMB (PAGE 152);
HERB STEM SALT (PAGE 246); FLAVOR SIMPLE SYRUP;
SKEWERS FOR SHISH KABOBS; STOVETOP SMOKING

Broccoli *stems*

BROCCOLI STEM CHILE STIR-FRY (PAGE 155);
BROCCOLI STEM POPPED BLACK-EYED PEA SLAW (PAGE 196);
SALAD ADD; MINESTRONE OR ANY VEG SOUP; SAUTÉED WITH
APPLES AND ONIONS; BOIL RIGHT IN WITH PASTA OR RICE

Pasta water

PASTA WATER CACIO E PEPE (PAGE 151);
FORTIFY ANY PASTA SAUCE; USE TO THICKEN SOUP;
BLANCH VEGGIES IN IT; COOKING WATER FOR GRAINS

Leftover
rice

YESTERDAY'S FRIED RICE WITH KIMCHI (PAGE 157);
RICE LATKES; ANY KIND OF CROQUETTES; GRAIN SALAD WITH
ROASTED CHILES AND PEPITAS; USE TO THICKEN SOUP; DOSAS

Mushroom
STEMS

MUSHROOM STEM RISOTTO (PAGE 158);
MARINATED MUSHROOMS; MUSHROOM STUFFING;
USE IN PASTA SAUCE; ADD TO STEWS

fish
collars

FISH COLLAR CIOPPINO (PAGE 165);
GRILL 'EM, BROIL 'EM, ROAST 'EM; ADD TO FISH STOCK;
FISH CHOWDER; BOUILLABAISSE

Pancetta *ends*

CLAMS AND BUCATINI WITH PANCETTA ENDS (PAGE 166);
ADD TO MAC AND CHEESE OR OTHER CASSEROLES; MAKE
BRUSCHETTA; USE AS A BASE FOR SOUPS; SERVE WITH EGGS,
ANYPLACE YOU WOULD SERVE BACON

Mustard dregs

MUSTARD DREGS CHICKEN BREASTS (PAGE 178);
BASE FOR SALAD DRESSING; MUSTARD CREAM REDUCTION;
HEARTY MARINADE; SAUCE UP YOUR PICKLES

Carrot
tops

CHUCK EYE WITH CARROT TOP SALSA VERDE (PAGE 147);
RADIATORE WITH CARROT TOP PESTO (PAGE 148); SUBSTITUTE FOR
PARSLEY; GARNISH; SALAD GREEN; SALAD DRESSING

Beef Shin OVEN BOLOGNESE

My dad doesn't eat swine, so whenever we go out for Italian he always asks if the restaurant adds pork fat to their ragù. Most do, because it's frigging delicious. But I guarantee you'll never miss it in this scrappy pork-free sauce, 'cause the meat you're using holds a flavor bomb in its core—super-rich bone marrow. It melts into the sauce, delivering all the creamy richness of rendered pork fat. **SERVES 8**

2 big bone-in beef shins, *aka shanks* cut like osso buco, between 2 and 3 pounds total

Lots of coarse sea salt and fresh ground black pepper

2 tablespoons olive oil

2 ribs celery *Use the leaves!*

1 medium onion, peeled and chopped

2 carrots, cut into small chunks *peels included*

4 garlic cloves, smashed and chopped

1 ½ cups *full-bodied* red wine

1 (14.5-ounce) can tomato puree

1 ½ cups beef stock, homemade or bought

1 ½ pounds scrappy pasta *Scraps from homemade pasta or broken-up lasagna noodles*

Lots of fresh grated Parmesan cheese, about 2 cups

Turn the oven to 350°F.

Season the beef shanks with plenty of salt and pepper. Pour the oil in a large Dutch oven and get it hot over high heat. Brown the shins, about 5 minutes per side. Remove from the pot. *Put the browned shanks on the upside-down lid of your Dutch oven, so it catches all the tasty juices.*

Turn the heat down to medium-low. Add the veggies and some more S&P and cook until they lose their raw look, about 10 minutes. Pour in the wine, tomato puree, and stock and get it boiling. Put the shins back in the pot, add the juices from the lid (and a Parm rind if you have it), cover, and throw in the oven until the meat is completely falling apart and the sauce smells amazing, about 3 hours. *Go do something fun while everything is simmering.*

Check the sauce. If it's a little thin, remove the lid and cook for another 30 minutes. Remove the Parm rind. If it's still cheesy, save for the next time you make sauce.

Shred the meat from the bones with a fork and lift out the bones (*use for stock*). If any marrow is still in the bones, push it out into the sauce with the handle end of a spoon.

Boil a lot of water in a big pasta pot. Add a couple handfuls of salt. *Don't be shy. Pasta water should have the salinity of seawater.* Throw in the pasta pieces, stir once, and boil until barely tender, about 3 minutes if fresh, 10 minutes if dried.

Remove the pasta with a handheld strainer or big slotted spoon and dump it into the sauce. Toss to coat. Don't worry if some pasta water gets in the sauce; the starch in the water will make the pasta sauce creamy. Serve tossed with fresh grated Parm.

Leftover Scraps

Onion skin—stock, veg soup, Onion Skin Fried Pickles (page 101)

Garlic paper—seasoning, stock

Beef bones—stock

CHUCK EYE WITH Carrot Top SALSA VERDE

One of the cheapest and best cuts of beef is chuck eye, which has all the flavor of chuck with the tenderness of sirloin. Here it's sauced with salsa verde, using carrot tops instead of parsley—gorgeous on pretty much anything! **SERVES 4**

2 pounds chuck eye steak or skirt steak, no more than 3/4 inch thick

2 tablespoons grapeseed oil or other mild-tasting oil

Coarse sea salt and coarsely ground black pepper

2 cups carrot tops

1 cup fresh basil leaves

1 cup fresh mint leaves

5 anchovies (half 2-ounce can)

Oil from the can of anchovies or other strong-tasting oil such as extra-virgin olive oil *Refill the half-emptied anchovy can with olive oil to get another batch of anchovy oil for next time.*

2/3 cup extra-virgin olive oil

1 teaspoon honey

Finely grated zest and juice of 1/2 lemon

Start by setting up your grill for high heat. Oil up the top side of your steaks and season with lots of salt and pepper. Slap your steaks, oil-side down, onto the grill. Season with more S&P and a little more oil and let them really char, about 3 minutes per side for medium-rare, a minute less or a few minutes more for rarer or more well-done. Take your steaks off the grill and let them rest.

While the steaks are resting, blitz your carrot tops, basil, mint, anchovies, anchovy oil, olive oil, honey, lemon juice, and lemon zest in a food processor. Once smooth, season with S&P and pour into a bowl.

If you want, while the grill is still hot, oil the cut surface of the lemon half and char it.

Slice the steaks against the grain, squeeze any juice remaining in the lemon over the steaks, and plate with a generous amount of the carrot top salsa verde.

Leftover Scraps

Squeezed lemon—Preserved Squeezed Lemons (page 253), grilled lemon garnish

Herb stems—Herb Stem Salt (page 246), seasoning, pesto

RADIATORE WITH Carrot Top PESTO

No one makes better pesto than my wife, Angiolina. She learned from her mom, and they were kind enough to pass the recipe (if not the pesto genes) down to me. Mine is not all basil. It has its own scrappy twist. **SERVES 4**

Coarse sea salt

1 pound radiatore pasta

Tops from 2 bunches carrots (stems and all), chopped coarse (about 2 cups)

1 cup fresh basil leaves and stems

2 garlic cloves, chopped

1/4 cup chopped toasted blanched almonds

About 1/2 cup extra-virgin olive oil

1/2 cup fresh grated Parmesan cheese

Fresh ground black pepper

Put a big pasta pot of water over high heat. Add a couple of handfuls of salt. *Don't be shy. Pasta water should have the salinity of seawater.* Add the pasta, stir once, and cook to al dente, about 10 minutes.

While the pasta is cooking, pack the carrot tops, basil, garlic, and almonds in a food processor. Pulse until everything is finely chopped but not mushy. Turn on the processor and drizzle the oil through the feed tube until the pesto is creamy and about the thickness of mayonnaise. *You may have a couple of tablespoons of oil left.*

Pulse a small ladle of pasta water and half the cheese into the sauce. Season with pepper and more salt if it needs it.

Drain the pasta, toss with the pesto and the rest of the Parm, and serve.

Leftover Scraps

Garlic paper—seasoning, stock

Pasta Water CACIO E PEPE

A part of me dies every time someone drains their pasta water and its magic disappears down the drain. This Roman classic black pepper pasta captures the creaminess of pasta water in the scrappiest way. No dish does a better job of making the most out of nothing. **SERVES 2**

Coarse sea salt

8 ounces spaghetti

2 tablespoons unsalted butter

1 1/2 teaspoons coarsely ground black pepper

1 cup grated pecorino or Parmesan cheese

Put a big pasta pot of water over high heat. Add a couple of handfuls of salt. *Don't be shy. Pasta water should have the salinity of seawater.* Add the spaghetti, stir once, and cook to al dente, about 7 minutes.

Right before the pasta is ready, melt the butter in a large skillet with a ladleful of the pasta water. 💲 Add the pepper and cook until lightly thickened.

Lift the al dente pasta with tongs or a spider strainer into the skillet and toss with the sauce. Add 2 ladles of pasta water and cook until the sauce is just thick enough to coat the pasta. Remove from the heat and stir in about 3/4 cup of the cheese. Add a little more pasta water if it doesn't look saucy enough. Serve topped with the remaining 1/4 cup cheese. Eat right away.

Rosemary Stem GRILLED LAMB

The thick, sort-of-woody branches of rosemary make fragrant skewers. They flavor the pierced meat from the inside, giving it the piney floral aroma that is what rosemary is all about. Plus, I think they look dang sexy on the plate. **SERVES 4**

1 pound boneless lamb shoulder, cut into big chunks

12 long rosemary branches (a foot long if you can find them), leaves stripped

3 tablespoons saved rosemary leaves *You can freeze the leftover rosemary leaves. Throw them in boiling water first to keep their color.*

8 garlic cloves, smashed

2 lemons, zest grated fine, fruit quartered

2 blood oranges, zest grated fine, fruit quartered

Coarse sea salt and coarsely ground black pepper

1/4 cup extra-virgin olive oil

Start by setting up your grill for medium-high direct heat.

Thread the chunks of lamb on the rosemary branches, leaving a little space between the pieces. *Whittling a point on one end of the branches helps.*

On a large cutting board, mince the rosemary leaves, garlic, lemon and orange zest, salt, and pepper as fine as you can. Drizzle the oil over the chopped ingredients and mix with your fingers into a rough paste. Roll the lamb skewers in the mixture, using your hands to slather them up.

Put the skewers on the hot grill and cook until charred all over and the internal temperature reaches 135ºF, about 10 minutes total, turning two or three times.

Toss the citrus quarters in whatever dregs of the rosemary oil mixture is left and grill until charred. Squeeze over the lamb before eating.

Leftover Scraps

Garlic paper—seasoning, stock

Rosemary leaves—seasoning

Broccoli Stem CHILE STIR-FRY

When you peel broccoli stems of their tough rubbery skin, the inner flesh comes out. Peeled broccoli stem has always reminded me of water chestnuts, crunchy with a hint of sweetness. This stir-fry is a total weeknight dish that can be whipped out in 15 to 20 minutes tops. **SERVES 4**

1 large head broccoli

2 tablespoons vegetable oil

1 thumb-size piece ginger, chopped fine *no need to peel*

4 garlic cloves, smashed and chopped fine

1/2 to 1 Fresno or serrano chile, chopped fine *the heat is up to you*

8 ounces smoked tofu or extra-firm plain tofu, cut into 1-inch pieces

2 tablespoons honey

1 tablespoon soy sauce

Coarse sea salt

1/4 cup toasted walnut pieces, chopped rough

2 cups fresh basil leaves

1 teaspoon toasted sesame oil

1 tablespoon sesame seeds *white or black, your choice*

Prep the broccoli first. Peel the stems and slice into 1/2-inch-thick rounds. It's easiest to do this starting near the florets and working toward the base. The slices will look like canned water chestnuts. Rough chop the top florets into bite-size pieces. Make separate piles of stems and florets.

Heat the vegetable oil in a large skillet over medium heat. Add the ginger, garlic, and chile and cook for about 30 seconds, until everything smells fantastic. Throw in the broccoli stems and 1/2 cup water. Simmer for a few minutes, until most of the water has evaporated. Add the broccoli tops and tofu.

Cook for another few minutes, stirring once in a while.

Turn the heat down to low and stir in the honey, soy sauce, and a little salt. Cook until the tofu is golden and a little glazed. Fold in the walnuts and basil. Drizzle with the sesame oil, top with the sesame seeds, and serve.

Leftover Scraps

Garlic paper—seasoning, stock

Chile seeds—toast for seasoning

Basil stems—Herb Stem Salt (page 246), pesto, pasta sauce

Broccoli stem peels—toss with oil and roast till crispy

Yesterday's Fried Rice WITH KIMCHI

For those of you who make your own fried rice, you probably already know that stale cold rice makes the crunchiest, chewiest, and most tender fried rice on the planet. Fried leftover rice is a gateway scrap. Once you eat it you will never go fresh again. **SERVES ABOUT 4**

1 tablespoon vegetable oil

4 cups cooked cooled rice *Don't use fresh cooked rice here. You want it a day or two old. It will get crispier!*

Fine sea salt and fresh ground black pepper

4 scallions, sliced thin on a slant, green tops saved for garnish *Chop up the roots, too.*

3 garlic cloves, sliced thin

1 cup frozen peas *Let defrost on the counter while you prep the vegetables.*

1 cup kimchi, chopped rough and packed down

4 eggs, any size

4 small sheets toasted nori, crumbled or chopped *Those little packets of seaweed snacks are great.*

Put a large nonstick skillet or wok over high heat. Add half the oil.

Add the rice and salt and pepper. Give it a quick stir, and then let it sit for a few minutes to develop some crispy edges.

Throw in the scallion bottoms and roots, the garlic, and peas. Stir and toss till the peas are bright green, about 2 minutes. Add the kimchi and cook until just warmed through. Pile onto a plate.

Wipe out the skillet, put back on a burner over medium-high heat, and add the remaining oil. Crack the eggs into the skillet and fry for 1 minute. Cover and cook for another minute, or until the white is set.

Slip the eggs on top of the rice and top with seaweed and scallion greens. *Gorgeous!*

Leftover Scraps

Garlic paper—seasoning, stock

Egg shells—clarifying stock, deacidifying coffee

Pickle Juice–Brined PORK CHOPS

Have you ever brined anything before? I'm guessing once, maybe twice, or *most likely* never. Pickle juice is a great starting point. Brines are intimidating; pickle juice is not. Pour it over any meat and sit down while your chop or steak gets tender and flavorful. **SERVES 4**

4 (³/₄-inch-thick) bone-in pork chops

1 ¹/₂ cups dill pickle juice (liquid from a 24-ounce jar)

Coarse sea salt and fresh ground black pepper

2 tablespoons sunflower oil or other mild-tasting oil

16 fresh dill sprigs

Soak the pork chops in the pickle juice in the refrigerator for 3 hours or overnight, whichever fits your schedule. *A zip-top bag works great.*

Turn the oven to 350°F.

Pat the pork chops dry and season the heck out of them with salt and pepper. Pour the oil into a large cast-iron skillet and put over medium-high heat. Wait until the oil is shimmering. Press half the dill sprigs into one side of the pork chops. Put them in the hot oil dill-side down and cook until browned and crispy, about 3 minutes. Press the rest of the dill on the top side and flip.

Throw in the oven and bake until the meat springs back to a forceful poke, 145°F on an instant-read thermometer inserted through the end of the thickest chop into the center of the meat. Rest for 5 minutes before digging in, to give the tough coagulated meat fibers some time to relax.

Heart of the Butt TONNATO

Billy, my butcher in Brooklyn, told me about this cut. It's a piece of meat that lies in the center of a pork butt, separated by a layer of fat that wrecks the shape of the pork butt roast, so most butchers cut it out and take it home. It sells for the price of pork butt, *CHEAP!* which is too tough to roast, but not this baby. It's rich, it's tender, and roasts like a dream. **SERVES 4**

1/4 cup extra-virgin olive oil

2 tablespoons capers

2 pounds pork heart-of-the-butt

1/2 teaspoon ground coriander

1/2 teaspoon ground cumin

Coarse sea salt and fresh ground black pepper

1 egg, any size

Finely grated zest and juice of 2 lemons

2 garlic cloves

1 teaspoon Dijon mustard

1 (5-ounce) can tuna in olive oil *Don't drain.*

About 1/2 cup mild-tasting vegetable oil

2 radishes with greens, radishes sliced, greens left whole

1 rib celery with leaves, rib sliced, leaves left whole

Turn the oven to 375°F.

Put a large cast-iron skillet over medium-high heat. Add the olive oil, wait a beat, and add the capers. Fry until they swell and pop, about 5 minutes. Remove to a small bowl.

Season the pork with the coriander, cumin, and salt and pepper and brown in the hot skillet on one side, about 3 minutes. Flip the meat over and slip the skillet into the oven; roast until the interior is 145°F, about 25 minutes. *Test with an instant-read thermometer stuck through one end of the roast, into the center of the meat.*

While the meat is roasting, put the egg, lemon zest, lemon juice, garlic, and mustard in a food processor and blitz to combine.

Pour the oil from the tuna into a glass measuring cup and add enough vegetable oil to make 2/3 cup. With the processor running, slowly pour the oil through the feed tube and keep processing until a creamy sauce forms, about 1 minute. Add the tuna and blitz until smooth, about another minute.

When the roast is done, let it sit for 5 minutes or so. Spread two-thirds of the tonnato sauce over a platter. Slice the meat and lay it on top. Scatter the radishes, celery, and capers over everything. Serve the rest of the tonnato on the side.

Leftover Scraps

Egg shell—clarifying stock, deacidifying coffee

Garlic paper—seasoning, stock

Squeezed lemon—Preserved Squeezed Lemons (page 253)

Fish Collar CIOPPINO

Fish collars are the collarbones of big fish like cod, halibut, kingfish, or salmon. They are large and are attached to a helluva lot of delish fish that usually gets scrapped. **SERVES 4**

3 tablespoons extra-virgin olive oil

6 garlic cloves, chopped fine

3 ribs celery, leaves and all, split lengthwise and sliced thin

1/2 teaspoon red chile flakes

1 1/2 teaspoons fennel seeds

8 small ripe tomatoes on the vine, taken off the vine and cut in half

1 cup white wine *nothing too sweet*

Coarse sea salt and fresh ground black pepper

12 littleneck clams, the smallest you can find, closed tight

2 fish collars, split into 4 manageable pieces

12 scrubbed mussels, closed tight

More celery leaves, for garnish

Pour the oil into a large heavy pot with a tight-fitting lid. Put over medium heat. *Don't cover yet.* Add the garlic, celery, chile flakes, and fennel seeds. Crush the tomatoes through your fingers into the pot and cook until everything smells unbelievable, about 5 minutes.

Add the wine, 1 teaspoon salt, and about 1/2 teaspoon pepper, turn the heat to high, and bring to a boil, crushing any big pieces of tomato with a spoon as you stir. Turn down to a simmer, add 2 cups water, and cook until the tomatoes are pulpy, about 10 minutes.

While the broth is simmering, toss the clams with a big pinch of salt in a large bowl and cover with water. Set aside for 10 minutes. *to rid them of sand*

Lay the collars on top of the vegetables in the pot, raise the heat to medium-high, and cover with a lid to steam the fish, about 5 minutes.

Holding each piece of fish collar with tongs, use a soup spoon to scrape the meat off the bones into the stew. It's fine if some skin gets in, but try to fish out most of it. *pun intended* Discard the bones.

Add the clams to the pot, cover, and cook for 3 minutes. Add the mussels, cover, and cook for 5 more minutes, or until all of the shellfish is open. As always, boost the flavor with more S&P if you think it needs it. Garnish with a fistful of chopped celery leaves.

Leftover Scraps

Tomato vines—pasta sauce, stock

Garlic paper—seasoning, stock

CLAMS AND BUCATINI WITH **Pancetta Ends**

Ever notice that when delis get to the end of whatever they're slicing, the leftovers hit the trash? I always ask for the ends of turkey, pastrami, and, in this case, pancetta to up my cooking, reduce my food bill, and give the deli dude a good laugh. **SERVES 4**

20 littleneck clams

Coarse sea salt and fresh ground black pepper

4 ounces pancetta ends, cut into little chunks

1 pound bucatini

4 garlic cloves, peeled and sliced thin

1/2 serrano chile, sliced

2 whole anchovy fillets

1 small bunch fresh Italian (flat-leaf) parsley, chopped fine (chop the stems first, then the leaves) *Keep separate.*

1 1/2 cups white wine

2 tablespoons unsalted butter

1/2 cup finely grated Parmesan cheese

Juice of 1/2 lemon

Toss the clams with about a tablespoon of salt in a large bowl and cover with water. Set aside for 10 minutes. *to rid them of sand*

Put a big pasta pot of water over high heat. Add a couple handfuls of salt. *Don't be shy.*

Pasta water should have the salinity of seawater.

Put the pancetta in a large deep pan over medium-high heat and cook until most of its fat has melted and the meaty bits are starting to brown, about 7 minutes.

Drop the bucatini in the boiling pasta water, stir once, and cook until al dente, 8 to 10 minutes.

At the same time, add the garlic, chile, anchovies, and parsley stems to the pancetta pan and cook until it smells amazing, about 1 minute. Drain the clams and add to the pan. Add the wine, cover and steam until the clams open, 5 to 8 minutes.

When the bucatini is done, lift it out of the water with tongs or a spider strainer and drop into the clam pan. If the clams are opened before the bucatini is done, remove the pan from the heat, then return it once the bucatini is ready. Add half the parsley leaves and the butter and boil until a sauce forms. Feel free to add a ladle or two of pasta water if the mixture starts to look dry or oily.

Remove from the heat and toss in the remaining parsley and the cheese. Drizzle with the lemon juice. *Wow! It's beautiful.* Serve right away.

Leftover Scraps

Anchovy oil—aioli, frying, salad dressing

Garlic paper—seasoning, stock

Squeezed lemon—Preserved Squeezed Lemons (page 253), grilled lemon garnish

Halibut Cheek TACOS

I guess you could say I'm obsessed with halibut cheeks. They're totally overlooked, and they're a completely different texture from the well-known fillet, buttery and supple rather than dense and meaty. If your fish seller doesn't have them, you gotta let them know how good they are and that they should get them in now. **SERVES 4**

¼ medium red cabbage, sliced paper thin *If you've got a mandoline, this is a great time to use it.*

½ medium onion, peeled and chopped small

3 red radishes with greens, radishes shaved into thin slices and cut into thin strips, greens chopped fine

½ bunch fresh cilantro, stems and leaves (everything), chopped

Finely grated zest and juice of 1 lime, plus 1 lime, cut into 8 wedges, for serving

1 teaspoon honey

1 tablespoon coarse sea salt

1 teaspoon smoked paprika

1 teaspoon dried oregano

1 teaspoon ground coriander

1 teaspoon ground cumin

1 teaspoon ground turmeric

1 teaspoon fresh ground black pepper

4 halibut cheeks (about 1 ½ pounds), cut in half *They should be the size of large scallops.*

3 tablespoons mild-tasting vegetable oil, such as grapeseed

8 white corn tortillas

1 avocado, peeled, pitted, and sliced thin

Swig of hot sauce, if you want

Start by setting up your grill for medium-high direct heat.

Make a slaw by tossing the cabbage, onion, radishes with their greens, the cilantro, lime zest, lime juice, honey, and 1 teaspoon of the salt in a large bowl. Let it be.

Mix the spices with the remaining salt on a big plate. Coat the halibut pieces in the spice rub and coat with 2 tablespoons of the oil.

Oil the grill grate with the rest of the oil and grill the cheeks until browned and tender, about 3 minutes per side.

Blister the tortillas on the grill for 10 seconds per side.

Make the tacos by putting a halibut cheek in the center of a tortilla and top with a little pile of slaw and a few avocado slices. Serve with the lime wedges and some hot sauce, if you want more spice.

Leftover Scraps

Squeezed lime—pickled lime, grilled garnish

Onion skin—stock, veg soup, Onion Skin Fried Pickles (page 101)

Avocado pit and skin—nothin' to be done

Apple Core BUTTER ROASTED DUCK

Duck can be a little too fatty, but when you pair it with something tart and sweet, its natural richness can make your knees buckle. This version is simple: the apple butter counters the fattiness of the duck and the cider captures all of the goodness from the drippings in the pan. This is one easy win! **SERVES 2**

2 boneless Muscovy duck breasts

Coarse sea salt and fresh ground black pepper

2 tablespoons Apple Core Butter (page 249)

1/2 cup hard cider, lager beer, or white wine

4 thyme sprigs

Slash the skin on the duck breasts with a sharp knife in a crosshatch pattern, cutting through the skin and the fat beneath but not into the meat. Season all over with lots of salt and pepper.

Put a medium cast-iron pan over medium-low heat and warm the pan for a minute. Put the duck breasts into the pan skin side down and cook until the skin browns and almost all of the fat has melted, about 10 minutes. *Don't rush it, and really wait for as much fat to render out as you can.*

Turn the duck breasts skin-side up. Pour the fat out of the pan into a coffee cup. *When cooled, pour into a storage container and save in the refrigerator.*

Add the apple butter and cider to the pan and turn the heat up to high. As the liquid in the pan reduces, it will start to look like melted caramel. As soon as it does, add the thyme and start spooning the pan liquid over the duck. Keep cooking and spooning until the duck is barely firm to the touch, the skin is glossy, and the glaze in the pan is bubbling all over. Turn the duck skin-side down to really saturate the surface with the sticky caramelized glaze. Baste the meat side with the pan juices.

The finish may test your nerve. Don't be shy. I'm here. Trust me. To get the skin crispy, you're going to have to burn

it a bit. When the liquid is practically gone, watch and wait until the glaze starts to burn around the edges of the pan. Lift and take a peek; the skin should be dark mahogany brown. If it's just golden, let it go more.

Put the duck on a cutting board to rest for 5 minutes, and slice on an angle. The meat will be medium-rare and the skin will be deep brown and slightly crisp. If you think you want your duck better done, change your mind.

Leftover Scraps

Rendered duck fat—frying potatoes or anything else

SPATCHED TURKEY WITH Turkey Scrap Gravy

Can we be honest and admit that the little bag of giblets hiding inside a turkey usually ends up in the trash? I guess they're kinda gross, but those innards are full of flavor and can be the difference between an awkward family get-together and the best feast of the year. **SERVES 10**

One 10-to 12-pound turkey with giblets

1 bunch fresh tarragon, leaves chopped, stems reserved

1 cup (2 sticks) unsalted butter, softened at room temp

Coarse sea salt and fresh ground black pepper

$1/4$ cup all-purpose flour

$1/2$ cup apple brandy or Cognac

Using poultry shears or a heavy knife, remove the turkey backbone and wing tips. Use the heel of your hand to press down on the breastbone of the turkey to flatten it. *Opening up the turkey cuts roasting time in half.*

Throw the turkey bones, giblets, and tarragon stems in a big Dutch oven or small stockpot. *Some turkeys come with a neck. If yours does, throw that bad boy in your stockpot, too.* Cover with cold water by an inch or so and simmer until it tastes strong, about 2 hours. Strain into a clean pot.

Meanwhile, turn the oven to 500°F.

Put the turkey bone-side down in a roasting pan. Rub the turkey skin with the butter and season with lots of salt and pepper. Timing tip: Let your turkey rest at room temp for about 1 hour before roasting. Roast the turkey until the skin is golden brown, about 30 minutes. Turn the oven down to 350°F. Continue to roast, basting with the pan drippings every 30 minutes, for another 1 to 1 1/2 hours, until an instant-read thermometer inserted into thickest part of a thigh reads 165°F.

Remove the turkey from the oven and put it on a large cutting board to rest for about 20 minutes. *A rest period lets the steamy meat firm up so it slices a lot easier.*

Place the roasting pan directly over two burners on low heat (if roasting on a baking sheet, pour the drippings into a large skillet and put it over one burner). Stir in the flour and keep stirring until golden, about 5 minutes. *It should be the thickness of wet sand. If it's too dry, add a little butter; if it's too wet, add a little more flour.*

Turn off the heat and stir in the brandy. Turn the heat back to low and stir until the stuff in the pan looks like wet sand again. Slowly whisk in 4 cups of your turkey stock and simmer until thickened, about 10 minutes. Strain through a fine-mesh sieve *or a gold coffee filter.* Adjust the taste with S&P and keep warm.

Carve the turkey. Pour a little gravy on the bottom of a serving platter, top with the turkey, and scatter with the chopped tarragon. Serve with extra gravy on the side.

Leftover Scraps

Turkey bones—stock

Turned Wine FRIED CHICKEN

Turned wine isn't trash: it's natural vinegar. Soaking chicken in it helps the meat get super tender and gives it the tart-honey-musky flavor of wine grapes. In this simple recipe, the wine really comes through in every bite. Who needs a beer with their fried chicken? **SERVES 4**

4 chicken thighs (about 1 pound)

1 cup turned red wine, whatever you've got

1 tablespoon red wine vinegar

1 1/2 cups Wondra flour

Coarse sea salt and fresh ground black pepper

Mild-tasting vegetable oil, for frying

A small handful of herb sprigs, your choice

Put the chicken thighs in a zip-top bag with the turned wine and vinegar and refrigerate overnight.

In a bowl, season the flour with 2 teaspoons salt and 1/2 teaspoon pepper.

Heat 1 1/2 inches of oil in a deep skillet to 375°F.

Lift the chicken out of the wine and plop it in the flour. Turn to coat all over. Gently slip the flour-coated chicken into the oil *You don't want to get splashed.* and fry until golden brown and a thermometer inserted into

the meat registers 165°F, about 15 minutes, turning halfway through.

Take the chicken out of the skillet with tongs or a slotted spoon and put on a few folded paper towels to drain and cool a little. Season with more S&P.

Drop the herbs into the hot oil and fry until they pop, about 10 seconds. Take them out with tongs and put on the paper towels to cool for a second.

Serve the chicken with the crispy herbs crushed over the top.

SCRAPPY Green Sauce DRUMSTICKS

Growing up in Seattle, Vietnamese flavors were everywhere, so I was a hardcore Viet food fan by the time I was nine years old. Forget your typical Americano chicken drumstick and save all your herb scraps to rock out with this awesome Vietnamese version. **SERVES 4**

2 scallions, root to stem, chopped rough

4 cups herb scraps, stems, leaves, whatever (definitely use some cilantro and mint, but if you like basil or parsley, or even arugula or watercress, go for it) *I wouldn't use rosemary or thyme, going for Asian compatibility here.*

1 tablespoon fish sauce

2 garlic cloves, smashed

Finely grated zest and juice of 1 lime

1-inch piece ginger, smashed

2 teaspoons (or so) sriracha sauce

1 teaspoon light or dark brown sugar

1/2 cup mild-tasting vegetable oil, plus more for cooking

8 bone-in, skin-on chicken drumsticks

Coarse sea salt

Aleppo or other red chile flakes

Throw the scallions, all but a small handful of the herbs, the fish sauce, garlic, lime zest and juice, ginger, sriracha, and brown sugar in a food processor and pulse a couple of times to chop up the herbs. With the machine running, stream in the oil. *You are looking for a drizzly consistency.*

Slash through the skin of each chicken leg in a few places. Toss the chicken with half of the green sauce (about 1/2 cup) in a bowl. Soak the chicken at room temp for 1 hour or up to overnight in the fridge.

When you're ready to cook, turn the oven to 400°F.

Put about 1 tablespoon of oil in a big heavy cast-iron skillet and get it hot over medium-high heat. Take the chicken out the marinade, pat dry, and season with salt. *It's OK if a little of the green sauce is still there.* Nestle the chicken pieces in the skillet and cook until browned on all sides, about 8 minutes total. When the oven is up to temp, slip the skillet into the oven and roast until an instant-read thermometer stuck in the thickest part of the biggest drumstick reads 165°F to 175°F, about 25 minutes. *For crispier chicken, stick under the broiler for a few minutes.*

Pour the drippings from the pan into the unused green sauce and pour all but a few tablespoons over the bottom of a platter. Stack the chicken in the pool of sauce. Season with more salt.

Drizzle the remaining sauce over the top and scatter the rest of the herbs and some chile flakes over the top. Dig in.

Leftover Scraps

Garlic paper—seasoning, stock

Squeezed lime—pickled lime, grilled garnish

Mustard Dregs CHICKEN BREASTS

Let's be honest about boneless chicken breast recipes—most of them suck. Sure, my recipe has a few more steps and calls for skin-on boneless chicken breast (a special order at most markets), but considering the faultlessly crisped skin on these babies paired with the pungent dregs rescued from a mustard jar, these are, hands down, one of the best things you will ever eat. For your herbs, you can use tarragon and parsley, but carrot tops and celery leaves are scrappier. **SERVES 2**

2 tablespoons extra-virgin olive oil

2 skin-on boneless chicken breast halves *You can ask the butcher to remove the bones from bone-in breast, or do it yourself.*

Coarse sea salt and fresh ground black pepper

1 cup white wine, any type

Mustard dregs clinging to the inside of a spent jar of brown mustard *about a tablespoon*

2 tablespoons capers

½ cup chicken stock, homemade (page 244) or bought

2 tablespoons unsalted butter

A few fresh herbs, for garnish

Turn the oven to 400°F.

Put a medium cast-iron skillet over medium-high heat for a minute or two until it's pretty hot. Add the oil. *It should shimmer right away.*

Season the chicken on both sides with plenty of salt and pepper. Put the chicken in the hot oil, skin-side down. Put a piece of foil over the chicken and then some kind of heavy weight right on top. A saucepan with a heavy can stuck in it works fine. The weight makes the skin side of the chicken get super crispy and it equals out the thick and thin ends of the breasts, allowing them to cook evenly. Cook until the skin side is crispy, about 5 minutes. If you smell burning, turn the heat down a little. Man, I wish there

was some word that means the heat level between medium and medium-high. *That's what you want.*

When the oven is up to temp, take the weight and foil off, flip the chicken over, and stick the skillet in the oven to finish cooking (160°F on a thermometer), about 8 minutes.

Pour the wine into the mustard jar, twist on the lid, and shake the heck out of it so that all of the dregs come off the jar and get disbursed in the wine.

Take the chicken out of the skillet and put it on a cutting board to rest.

Put the skillet back over a high burner *Use a towel to grip the handle. It's hot!* and throw the capers into the fat in the pan.

Cook until they swell and pop, about 1 minute.

Pour the mustardy wine into the skillet. Add the chicken stock to the mustard jar, reseal, and shake again; pour into the skillet and boil until the liquid is almost all gone. What's left will be syrupy. Stir with a whisk to scrape up any browned bits clinging to the bottom of the skillet *Browned bits, the Ruler of Scraps!* and shake the skillet, especially near the end, to keep it from scorching. Take the skillet off the heat and whisk in the butter to make a sauce.

Pour the sauce on a serving plate. Slice the chicken breast, plate it, and pour on more sauce. Garnish with some flavorful green herbs.

Kitchen Sink *Upside-Down Skillet* Whey PIZZAS

Do you like sourdough? Do you like pizza? If both answers are yes, this is your baby. The natural tartness of whey from yogurt gives any pizza dough recipe a rocked-out sourdough vibe. The toppings are up to you. Use anything but the kitchen sink. **SERVES 6**

Dough

1 (¼-ounce) packet active dry yeast

1 ½ cups warm whey or hot tap water *Hot enough to shower in.*

1 ½ tablespoons honey

¼ cup extra-virgin olive oil, plus more for the bowl

About 4 cups all-purpose flour

2 teaspoons fine sea salt

Topping

Extra-virgin olive oil

Coarse sea salt and fresh ground black pepper

1 cup sauce *white, red, meat, whatever*

3 cups vegetable scraps, ends of roasted meat, fresh herbs, etc. 💲

1 cup shredded or crumbled cheese *Whatever you've got.*

To make the dough: Mix the yeast, whey, and honey in a measuring cup. Leave it alone until the mixture is bubbling, about 10 minutes. Stir in the ¼ cup of oil.

Mix 3 ¾ cups of the flour and the salt in the bowl of a standing mixer set up with a dough hook. Add the combined liquid ingredients and mix on medium speed until they form into a soft, pliable dough ball. If the dough stays too wet to become a ball, sprinkle it with the rest of the flour and, using your hands, push the flour down the sides of the bowl to release the wet dough.

Dump the dough out onto a board and knead for a few minutes, adding more flour if it feels sticky. Wash out the bowl and grease the inside of the bowl with a little more oil. Flip the dough back into the oiled bowl and cover with a towel. Let it hang until it is doubled in size, about 1 ½ hours. *When doubled, the impression of your finger stuck into the dough will stay there without filling back in.*

Turn the oven to 500°F. Dust a baking sheet with flour.

Put an upside-down large cast-iron skillet on the bottom rack of the oven. If you have two skillets, you'll be able to bake two pizzas at once.

Cut the dough into 6 pieces and form each piece into a ball. Put the balls on the prepared baking sheet. Throw a little more flour over each piece of dough. Cover with a towel and let hang for about 15 minutes.

For each pizza, put a big square of parchment paper on a cutting board. Spread the dough out with your fingers on the parchment. Once it is

about ¼ inch thick, flour the top and roll it out all the way using a wine bottle or rolling pin. Rub the top with oil and season liberally with S&P. Top with a portion of sauce, scraps, and cheese. Slip the pizza from its parchment square onto the bottom of the skillet in the oven.

When the oven is up to temp, bake until the dough is puffed and the bottom is well browned, about 8 minutes. Drizzle on more oil, cut into wedges, and eat.

Seven Killer Pizza Toppings

White sauce, kale stems, cured ham or sausage ends, egg

Smashed tomato seconds, bruised spinach, mozzarella, anchovy oil

White sauce, spent lemons, asparagus trimmings, sliced chiles, goat cheese

Meat sauce, leek tops, mozz

Ranch dressing, clams, potato trimmings, blue cheese

Carrot peels, pesto, mushroom ends, chile seeds

Red sauce, fennel trimmings, pepperoni ends

Washington Apples
Baker & Ringstad

sixteen

6

Beet stems

BEET GREENS WITH NUTMEG AND CLEMENTINE (PAGE 193);
RAW IN SALADS; WILTED IN SOUPS AND SAUCES;
SAUTÉED WITH GARLIC; STIR-FRIED

Radish tops

GLAZED RADISHES AND THEIR TOPS (PAGE 203);
MIX IN WITH SALAD GREENS; GOOSE UP A PESTO; ADD TO
PISTOU; SALSA VERDE (WHY NOT?); SCRAMBLED EGGS ADD-IN

Brussels *leaves*
sprouts FRANKENSPROUTS (PAGE 198);

USE AS A SPICY SALAD GREEN; BLEND INTO SOUPS;

BRUSCHETTA TOPPER; FRIED LIKE CHIPS AND DIPPED

Zucchini ends

ZUCCHINI ENDS WITH BUTTER BEANS (PAGE 201);
FOLD INTO A FRITTATA; TOSS WITH PASTA OR RISOTTO;
ADD TO MINESTRONE; ROAST 'EM

Whole Cauliflower GRATIN

If you look closely at a head of cauliflower, you will notice big chop marks where the greens were. Cauliflower has the most luscious, incredibly delicious greens. Tell your produce seller that you want them, or at least you don't want them hacked off the cauliflowers you buy. This gratin puts whole cauliflower on center stage, stems, core, leaves, and all. **SERVES 4**

2 tablespoons unsalted butter

4 garlic cloves, chopped fine

Small handful whole fresh sage leaves (about 20 leaves)

2 tablespoons all-purpose flour

1 cup heavy cream

4 ounces fresh goat cheese, *aka chèvre* in pieces

1/2 whole nutmeg, grated

Coarse sea salt and fresh ground black pepper

1 head cauliflower with leaves and core

1 cup finely shredded Parmesan cheese

1 teaspoon Aleppo or other red chile flakes

Turn the oven to 400°F.

Put a medium cast-iron skillet over medium heat. Add the butter, garlic, and sage and cook gently until the butter melts. *Your house is going to smell insane.* Add the flour and stir until incorporated. Cook for 1 minute; keep stirring. Pour in the cream; keep stirring. When it thickens, remove from the heat and stir in the goat cheese until it is mostly combined. *It's OK if it's a little lumpy.* Season with the nutmeg and a good amount of S&P.

Cut the stem/core off the bottom of the cauliflower. Pluck the leaves off the head and cut the leaves into small pieces.

Slice the core into paper-thin rounds, like chips. Cut the cauliflower head into thin slices like you're slicing a loaf of bread. Toss everything into the skillet so that the cauliflower pieces are evenly coated with the cheese and cream. Pack the top down with your hands.

Sprinkle the top with the Parmesean cheese, red chile flakes, and more S&P. When the oven is up to temp, bake until the cauliflower is fork-tender and the casserole is browned and bubbling, about 45 minutes.

Leftover Scraps

Garlic paper—seasoning, stock

Beef Fat SPUDS

I started making these for my dad's family on Friday nights for Shabbat. It's our family favorite. No potato recipe out there compares. **SERVES 4**

8 Yukon Gold potatoes, peeled and cut in half *Save the peels to make Spicy Potato Skin Crisps (page 113)*

2 tablespoons beef fat, aka tallow (page 257)

1 teaspoon sea salt, plus more for finishing

Turn the oven to 400°F.

Put the potatoes on a rimmed baking sheet, pour in 1 cup water, and cover the pan with foil. When the oven is up to temp, bake until the potatoes look cooked but are still firm, about 20 minutes. Remove the foil and drain off the water.

Roughly toss the potatoes with the beef fat and salt so that the edges of the potatoes look frayed. *You want to rough them up to make lots of edges that can get crisp.* Bake for another hour, stirring every 15 minutes or so, until the outsides are brown 'n crispy. Season with more salt and serve.

Leftover Scraps

Potato peels—Spicy Potato Skin Crisps (page 113)

Beet Greens WITH NUTMEG AND CLEMENTINE

Don't throw out your beet greens. They're exactly the same thing as chard. And don't bypass the stems. They are super creamy and tasty. **SERVES 4**

1 tablespoon vegetable oil

1 garlic clove, smashed

1/2-inch piece ginger, chopped fine *Crush your ginger with the side of a knife before chopping*

1/2 fresh red chile, sliced thin

1 preserved lemon, homemade (see page 253) or bought, chopped fine

Zest and juice of 2 clementines *Clementines don't have pith, so there's not much waste.*

Coarse sea salt and fresh ground black pepper

1 pound beet greens (from about 2 bunches beets), including stems, chopped *Stems add a little crunch to cooked greens*

1/4 teaspoon ground or grated nutmeg *about 5 gratings on a grater*

Put a big skillet over medium heat. Add the oil, wait a beat, then add the garlic, ginger, and chile. Stir until you can smell the ginger and garlic and the chile fumes make you cough a little, about 1 minute.

Add the preserved lemon, clementine zest, and 1 teaspoon salt. Stir in the greens, cover the skillet, and cook until the greens wilt, about 8 minutes.

Add the nutmeg and clementine juice. Season with more salt and some pepper. Time to eat!

Leftover Scraps

Garlic paper—seasoning, stock

SWEET Corn Cob GRITS

Making use of corn cobs to flavor a broth is one of the easiest wins in the kitchen. It gives a natural sweetness than no one can pin down. Your cooking is about to completely change. **SERVES 4**

3 bare naked corn cobs, snapped in half

2 cups milk *I like whole milk, but use what you've got.*

Coarse sea salt

1 tablespoon granulated sugar

1 cup stone-ground white grits

Fresh ground white or black pepper

2 tablespoons unsalted butter

1½ cups grated sharp white cheddar cheese

Put the corn cobs, 1 quart water, the milk, ½ teaspoon salt, and the sugar in a large saucepan and simmer until the liquid is flavorful, about 20 minutes. Strain 4 cups into a medium heavy-bottomed Dutch oven, put over high heat, and run laps till it boils.

Whisk in the grits and turn down to a simmer. Simmer until thick, about 30 minutes, stirring about every 5 minutes. Stir in the pepper, butter, and cheese. *And more salt if you think it needs it.* Eat 'em quick before they lose their heat.

Leftover Scraps

Corn stock—Sweet corn drinks (atol de elote, chicha morada), corn soup, liquid for baking

Broccoli Stem *Popped Black-Eyed Pea* SLAW

I wanted to make a slaw that was more like a main course. I've always felt that broccoli stems have so much more personality and oomph than cabbage. Toss in some popped black-eyed peas for protein and it's all you need. **SERVES 4**

Slaw

- 1 tablespoon canola oil or other mild-tasting vegetable oil
- 1 (14.5-ounce) can black-eyed peas, drained and shaken dry
- 1 teaspoon garlic powder
- 2 big heads broccoli, with long stems still on them
- 1/2 red onion, peeled and chopped fine
- 3/4 cup roasted unsalted peanuts

Dressing

- 1 tablespoon honey
- 1 tablespoon Dijon mustard
- 1/2 cup apple cider vinegar
- 1 teaspoon celery seeds
- 1/2 cup canola oil
- 2 teaspoons fine sea salt
- Swig of hot sauce, if you want

Put the oil in a large skillet *I like cast-iron.* and put over medium heat. Add the black-eyed peas and garlic powder. Cook until crispy and blistered, about 6 minutes, stirring most of the time.

Shave the florets off the top of the broccoli with a knife like you're giving the broccoli a haircut. It should look like a pile of green vegetable couscous. Shred the broccoli stems on the coarse teeth of a box grater.

Mix the shredded stems, shaved broccoli head, crispy black-eyed peas, and red onion in a big bowl. Wrap the peanuts in a flat-weave kitchen towel and bang with a hammer to crush. Add half of the peanuts to the slaw.

Put all the dressing ingredients in a jar, seal it, and shake. Pour over the broccoli stem mixture and toss everything together.

Put in the fridge for at least 1 hour to marinate, then serve topped with the remaining peanuts.

Leftover Scraps

Onion skins—stock, veg soup, Onion Skin Fried Pickles (page 101)

Frankensprouts

Most people cut the bottoms off Brussels sprouts and throw them away along with all the loose leaves. As you now know, I love to take advantage of trashed bits like these. This sheet roast totally messes with your senses in all the right ways. **SERVES 4**

3 cups (12 ounces) whole Brussels sprouts

1 lime

1 teaspoon Asian fish sauce

1/2 stick (4 tablespoons) unsalted butter

1 teaspoon honey

1 teaspoon crushed red chile flakes

Coarse sea salt and fresh ground black pepper

Turn the oven to 425°F.

Trim the sprouts: Cut off the bottoms, let any loose leaves fall, and halve the trimmed sprouts. Arrange the 3 parts (bottoms, loose leaves, and halved sprouts) on a rimmed baking sheet, giving each part its own space.

Grate the zest off of the lime. Cut the lime in half and squeeze the juice into a small bowl. Stir in the fish sauce and stick it aside. Chop up the juiced lime carcass.

Melt the butter in a small saucepan over low heat and stir in the lime zest.

Toss the chopped lime with the Brussels sprouts bottoms.

Toss the leaves with the honey. Pour the butter over each of the sprout piles and toss to coat. Make sure the parts stay separated. Sprinkle the chile flakes and salt and pepper over everything.

Roast for 20 to 25 minutes, until the leaves are charred and crispy, the bottoms are fork-tender but still chewy, and the halved sprouts are caramelized and tender.

To serve, toss the bottoms and halved sprouts in a bowl with the lime juice–fish sauce mixture. Top with crisped leaves. Go at it.

Zucchini Ends WITH BUTTER BEANS

The first thing anyone does to a zucchini is knock off the top and the bottom. What the . . . ? Those ends are so dang delicious, and they're exactly the same thing as the rest of the zucchini. *We gotta stop wasting food!* **SERVES 4**

About 1 cup (8 ounces) dried butter beans *large lima beans*

¼ cup extra-virgin olive oil,

4 zucchini tops and bottoms or 1 whole zucchini, cut into big chunks

1 medium onion, peeled and cut into medium chunks

4 garlic cloves, sliced thin

1 teaspoon fennel seeds

2 teaspoons dried oregano

1 teaspoon Aleppo or other red chile flakes

Coarse sea salt and fresh ground black pepper

Finely grated zest and juice of 2 lemons

3 ounces feta cheese

Soak the beans in plenty of water overnight. Drain, dump into a big saucepan, and cover with fresh water. Put over medium-high heat. Bring to a boil and remove the foam from the top. Turn down the heat and simmer until the beans are tender, about 45 minutes. Drain. *Can be done up to 24 hours ahead.*

Turn on the broiler.

Put a large cast-iron skillet or any skillet that can go under the broiler (it can't have a plastic handle) over medium-high heat. Pour in 3 tablespoons of the oil, wait a beat, and add the zucchini to brown. Don't stir too much; you want these little guys to get crispy and delicious. When they're browned on one or two sides, *It'll take about 6 minutes, stirring once* add the onion, garlic, fennel seeds, oregano,

red chiles flakes, and S&P and cook until the onion is tender, stirring every now and then, about 5 more minutes.

Stir in the lemon zest and juice and crumble the cheese over the top. Drizzle with the last tablespoon of olive oil. Stick it under a broiler long enough to brown the cheese, about 5 minutes.

Leftover Scraps

Squeezed lemon—Preserved Squeezed Lemons (page 253), grilled lemon garnish

Onion skin—stock, veg soup, Onion Skin Fried Pickles (page 101)

Garlic paper—seasoning, stock

GLAZED RADISHES *and Their Tops*

My little sister Erin requests radishes and wilted greens every birthday. By glazing the radishes while you're cooking the greens, you kill two birds with one stone. **SERVES 4**

2 tablespoons unsalted butter

2 bunches radishes, tops
separated, curly roots on
*I like the radish bulbs split
lengthwise*

1 1/2 teaspoons salt

Finely grated zest and juice
of 1 lemon

1/2 teaspoon fresh grated nutmeg

Melt the butter in a big skillet over medium heat. Throw in the split radishes and salt. Cook until starting to brown but still crisp-tender, about 5 minutes, stirring a lot.

Add the radish tops, lemon zest and juice, and nutmeg. Turn the heat down to low, cover, and cook until the greens wilt and the radishes are tender, about 3 more minutes.

Leftover Scraps

Squeezed lemon—Preserved Squeezed Lemons (page 253), grilled lemon garnish

7

Dessert

Spent coffee

SPICE RUBS; COFFEE-FLAVORED SALT AND SUGAR;

MILK SHAKES; BARBECUE SAUCE.

STRAWBERRY
tops

STRAWBERRY TOP SHORTCAKE (PAGE 221);
STRAWBERRY PRESERVES; STRAWBERRY DESSERT SAUCE;
STRAWBERRY SIMPLE SYRUP; STRAWBERRY VINEGAR

Stale potato CHIPS

STALE POTATO CHIP CHOCOLATE CHIP COOKIES (PAGE 225);
BREADING FOR CHICKEN; SALAD TOPPER; MIGAS; NACHOS

Spent grain

SPENT GRAIN GRAHAM CRACKERS (PAGE 235);
ADD TO BREAD DOUGH; MAKE DINNER ROLLS; HEALTHY BISCOTTI;
FORTIFY FRY BATTER; SPECKLE UP YOUR WAFFLES; MALTED SHORTBREAD

Bruised
pears

BRUISED PEAR PANDOWDY (PAGE 232);
FRUIT SAUCE; PIE; SORBET; PUDDING; SMOOTHIE

Basil Stem PANCOTTA with Figs

The first time I picked basil everything smelled of basil even though I hadn't touched a leaf. All of that aroma was coming from the stems. Anything the leaf can do the stems can do just as well. This basil-scented panna cotta (one of my favorite desserts) is dished up family style—way easier than pouring it into individual molds. **SERVES 6**

1 packet (1/4 ounce) unflavored
   gelatin

4 stalks basil, 8 leaves saved

1 3/4 cups heavy cream

1 cup milk

1/2 cup plus 2 tablespoons
   granulated sugar

1/2 teaspoon salt

Fresh figs, cut into rounds

Put the gelatin and 1/4 cup cold water in a small bowl and stir with your fingers. *Scrappiest tool you have.* Set aside to soften for 5 minutes or so.

Crush the basil stalks (leaves and stems, except for the saved leaves) with your hands to bruise them and put them in a large heavy saucepan with the cream, milk, 1/2 cup of the sugar, and the salt; cook over medium heat, stirring every now and then, just long enough to simmer. Remove from the heat and let the mixture hang for 10 minutes to cool down.

Whisk in your softened gelatin. Really whisk it good so the gelatin disperses. Strain into a shallow 1-quart serving bowl. Refrigerate until set, about 3 hours.

About 30 minutes before you're ready to eat, toss the cut figs with the remaining sugar.

To serve, scatter the figs over the panna cotta. Tear the saved basil leaves into small pieces and scatter over all. Dish up.

Spent Coffee ICE CREAM

On our third date, Angiolina whipped out homemade coffee ice cream that I still think about to this day. What made it stand out for me was the little flecks of ground coffee. I adored the texture, and I love any food that's naturally this scrappy. **SERVES 4**

1 cup half-and-half

2 cups heavy cream

3/4 cup granulated sugar

1 cup packed spent coffee grounds 💲

6 large egg yolks

1/4 teaspoon fine sea salt

Stir the half-and-half, cream, and sugar in a medium saucepan and put over medium heat. When it simmers, stir in the coffee grounds, remove from the heat, cover, and steep until fully flavored, about 20 minutes.

Meanwhile, whisk the egg yolks in a large bowl until thick. Whisk a ladle or two of the warm coffee-cream mixture into the egg yolks. Now slowly pour the yolks into the pot of cream, whisking the whole time. Cook over low heat, stirring all the time, until the custard is barely thick enough to coat the back of a spoon. *If you use a candy thermometer, it will register 170°F.* Stir in the salt. Strain through a fine-mesh sieve. *A gold coffee filter works great.*

Pour into a bowl and put in a bigger bowl of ice water. Stir until the ice cream mixture is cool to the touch. Cover and refrigerate for at least 4 hours, until completely cold. *Do it a day ahead so the custard is really cold before churning into ice cream.*

Churn according to the ice cream machine manufacturer's directions. Eat right away, or store in a tightly closed container in the freezer, but not for more than a day.

Leftover Scraps

Egg whites—meringue, soufflé, cookies, cakes, egg white omelet

Egg shells—clarifying stock, deacidifying coffee

Pineapple Core FOSTER

I'm ripping off bananas Foster here, people! If you're unfamiliar, that's the flaming tableside treat made by the guy in the penguin suit with the singed eyebrows. It's an easy go-to. Utilizing the cores that get ripped out of pineapples lends this scrappy variation on the classic planetary cred. **SERVES 4 TO 6**

1/2 stick (4 tablespoons) unsalted butter, cut into chunks

2/3 cup packed dark brown sugar

1 vanilla bean, split lengthwise, seeds scraped out *Don't throw out the pod.* $

12 green cardamom pods, crushed *Bang 'em with the bottom of a heavy glass or a saucepan.*

Core from a ripe pineapple *The bottom should yield a little and smell strongly of pineapple* sliced thin

1/2 cup brandy

1 quart dulce de leche ice cream or your favorite ice cream

Crushed butter cookies or piecrust, for garnish (if you want) *Save your pie scraps and bake them into little cookies.*

Put a heavy medium skillet over medium-high heat. *Cast-iron is great for this.* Add the butter and brown sugar and stir until the butter melts and everything is well mixed and bubbling. Add the vanilla pod and seeds, cardamom pods and seeds, and sliced pineapple. Cook, stirring, until the sugar completely dissolves and the fruit is coated with sauce, about 1 minute.

Remove from the heat and pour in the brandy. *It might flame up. Don't freak. Just cover the pan with a lid and the flames will go out.* Put the skillet back over medium-high heat and simmer for about 3 minutes, stirring to keep it from burning. Turn the heat to low and simmer until the sauce thickens a little, about 5 more minutes, stirring when you want.

Serve everyone a couple of scoops of ice cream. Spoon pineapple and sauce over top. Garnish with cookies or piecrust crumbs, if using.

Leftover Scraps

Pineapple scraps—infuse into spirits or vinegar

Bloomed Chocolate *Malt* MUG CAKE

You know what bloomed chocolate is. You've seen it when you find that candy bar with white chalky stuff all over it that's been in the back of the drawer for years. Most people think it's moldy or gone bad, but it's perfectly fine. All that's happened is the cocoa butter has separated from the rest of the chocolate. Don't use it to feed the garbage can. Feed yourself. **SERVES 4**

1 stick (8 tablespoons) unsalted butter *Save the wrappers to butter the dishes.*

¼ cup demerara or raw sugar, for coating the mugs

6 ounces bloomed bittersweet chocolate, cut into chunks

1 teaspoon coffee grounds *Can use spent coffee. If you do $*

¼ cup chocolate malt powder *such as Ovaltine Classic Malt*

2 large eggs

2 large egg yolks

¼ cup granulated sugar

2-finger pinch of fine sea salt

Your favorite ice cream, for serving

Turn the oven to 350°F.

Line four 6-ounce mugs with butter and sprinkle with demerara sugar. *Adds a nice crunch.*

Melt the butter and chocolate with the coffee grounds in a double boiler over simmering water. *Helpful Hack: Set a heatproof bowl over a saucepan of simmering water.* Remove the top of the double boiler from the water and stir in the malt powder.

Beat the eggs, egg yolks, granulated sugar, and salt in a medium bowl until thick and pale, using a whisk and your big guns. Quickly fold the melted chocolate into the beaten eggs. Spoon the batter into the prepared mugs. Put on a baking sheet and bake just long enough to set the centers, about 35 minutes. Let the cakes cool in the mugs for 3 to 5 minutes before serving up, topped with ice cream.

Leftover Scraps

Egg whites—meringue, soufflé, cookies, cakes, egg white omelets

Egg shells—clarifying stock, deacidifying coffee

Strawberry Top SHORTCAKE

Nobody loves berries more than my mom. She slices them up every morning and eats a giant bowlful. And every morning there's a pile of strawberry tops in the sink. One morning I decided to play with them. I guess you could say I haven't looked back. **SERVES 6**

Strawberries

1 1/2 pounds (about 5 cups) strawberries, tops cut off and saved, large berries quartered, smaller berries cut in half

1 cup granulated sugar

1/2 cup Riesling (or another semisweet wine)

1/2 vanilla bean, seeds scraped, pod saved

Shortcakes

1 1/4 cups all-purpose flour

3/4 cup fine cornmeal, plus more for the board

1 tablespoon baking powder

1 teaspoon fine sea salt

1/3 cup granulated sugar

1 1/2 cups heavy cream, plus more for brushing on top

2 cups sweetened whipped cream, for assembly

To make the strawberries: Mix the strawberry tops, sugar, wine, and 1 cup water in a medium saucepan and put over medium heat. Simmer until lightly thickened, about 15 minutes. Remove from the heat and add the vanilla bean and scraped vanilla seeds. Cover and steep for 20 minutes. Strain and pour the syrup over the cut strawberries into a medium bowl. *Rinse off the vanilla bean, let dry, and reuse.*

Turn the oven to 425°F.

Line a baking sheet with a silicone baking mat or parchment paper.

To make the shortcakes: Mix the flour, cornmeal, baking powder, salt, and sugar in a large bowl. Stir in the heavy cream with a wooden spoon until a shaggy dough forms.

Gather into a ball and turn out onto a clean work surface sprinkled with cornmeal.

Pat the dough out to about 3/4 inch thickness. Cut into 6 squares. Put on a baking sheet evenly spaced and brush the tops with a little cream. Bake until puffed and golden brown, about 30 minutes. Cool for 10 minutes before assembling.

To assemble, cut the shortcakes in half horizontally. Fill with the strawberries, whipped cream, and a drizzle of syrup. Top with more whipped cream.

Leftover Scraps

Scraped vanilla pod—vanilla sugar, flavoring custards, tea

Wrinkled Blueberry CROSTATA

Wrinkled blueberries are what you get when you buy a boatload of blueberries on sale, hide them in the back of the refrigerator, and forget that you have them. You may think they're toast, but they've actually just been hanging out, getting rid of moisture, and concentrating their flavor on their way to being laced into muffins, pancakes, and rustic crostatas like this one. **SERVES 6 TO 8**

Crust

1 1/2 cups all-purpose flour, plus more for the board

1 tablespoon granulated sugar

1/2 teaspoon fine sea salt

1 stick (8 tablespoons) cold unsalted butter, sliced thin

1/3 cup plus 1 tablespoon cold buttermilk, plus more for brushing on the crust

Demerara or raw sugar, for the top of the crust *A couple of packets "borrowed" from the coffee shop is plenty.*

Filling

2 cups blueberries *wrinkled, squished . . . they all work*

1/4 cup granulated sugar

Finely grated zest and juice of 1 clementine

2 tablespoons all-purpose flour

2-finger pinch of fine sea salt

Confectioners' sugar, for dusting

To make the crust: Mix the flour, granulated sugar, and salt in a large bowl. Add the butter and pinch it into small pieces with your fingertips until the pieces of butter are the size of split peas. *Alternatively, freeze your butter and shred it on the large teeth of a box grater.*

Mix in the buttermilk, using a fork to form a shaggy dough. Dump it out onto a floured work surface and gently press into a large blob. Flatten into a 3/4-inch-thick square (this will make it easier to roll out later), wrap in plastic, and refrigerate for at least 1 hour. The pie dough can be refrigerated for several days before rolling it out to form a crust. *The dough may need 10 minutes at room temp before rolling out.*

While the dough is chilling, make the filling: Mix the blueberries, granulated sugar, clementine zest and juice, flour, and salt in a big bowl. Let it hang for about 10 minutes. *This is called maceration, and it makes berries juicy.*

Turn the oven to 400°F.

Roll the dough into a 12 × 18-inch rectangle that's about 1/4 inch thick and slip it onto a flat baking sheet. *It will cover the sheet.* Spread the blueberries and any accumulated juices down the center of the crust, leaving a 2-inch border. Fold and pleat the uncovered crust over the edge of the blueberries, leaving a line of fruit still showing down the center. Brush the crust with a little buttermilk and sprinkle everything with demerara sugar. *Sparkle and crunch!*

Bake for about 1 hour, until the crust is golden brown. Let cool for about 10 minutes. Dust the top with confectioners' sugar, cut, and serve.

Leftover Scraps

Spent clementine skin and juiced flesh—flavor liquor or vinegar

Stale Potato Chip CHOCOLATE CHIP COOKIES

My brother Alex squishes chips into everything he eats. Totally inspired by him, I'm taking stale old potato chips and studding my chocolate chip cookies with them. Salty, crispy, naughty. **SERVES 6** *2 cookies per person*

2 sticks (16 tablespoons) unsalted butter, cut into chunks, softened at room temp

3/4 cup packed dark brown sugar

1/2 cup granulated sugar

2 large eggs

Seeds scraped from 1 vanilla bean *Save the pod for another recipe.*

3 cups plus 2 tablespoons all-purpose flour

1 teaspoon baking powder

1/4 teaspoon baking soda

1 1/2 teaspoons fine sea salt

2 cups (10 ounces) semisweet chocolate disks *Disks, unlike chips, give a layered effect to the cookies*

2 cups crushed stale ridged potato chips *plus a few to snack on*

Beat the butter in a stand mixer fitted with the paddle attachment on medium speed until smooth and creamy, about 2 minutes. Add both sugars and continue to beat until fluffy. Add the eggs and vanilla seeds and beat for a few more minutes, periodically scraping down the sides of the bowl.

Mix the flour, baking powder, baking soda, and salt in a medium bowl and spoon into the mixer. Beat on the lowest speed and scrape down the sides of the bowl until the batter is smooth, about 1 minute.

Add the chocolate disks and potato chips and beat on the lowest speed until just combined. *Do not overmix or you'll get potato dust instead of chips.* Pat the dough into a 2-inch-thick rectangle, wrap in plastic wrap, and refrigerate overnight. *Trust me on this. It really improves the texture of the cookies.*

Turn the oven to 375°F. Line a baking sheet with a silicone baking mat or parchment paper.

Cut the dough into 12 squares. *Square cookies are a bit different and play up the rustic look.* Put 6 cookies evenly spaced on the sheet. When the oven is up to temp, bake for about 20 minutes, until golden brown on the edges. *Do not overbake or you won't get a gooey center.* Let cool on the sheet for 2 minutes before moving to a wire rack to cool the rest of the way. Bake the next batch the same way.

Leftover Scraps

Scraped vanilla pod—vanilla sugar, flavoring custards, tea

Egg shells—clarifying stock, deacidifying coffee

Squished Plum ICEBOX MOUSSE

When you pick ripe stone fruit at the peak of summer there is always a bunch that are overripe and squishy. Look for these and buy them at a discount to make this retro frozen treat. **SERVES 8**

Nonstick cooking spray

12 ounces overripe red plums (about 4 large), pits removed, cut into chunks

2-inch piece ginger, peels and all, grated

1 cup granulated sugar

1/2 teaspoon fine sea salt

3 large egg whites

1 cup cold heavy cream

Coat a 9 × 5-inch loaf pan with nonstick cooking spray and line with plastic wrap with a few inches of overhang on all sides.

Toss the plums, ginger, 1/3 cup of the sugar, and the salt in a medium saucepan and put over high heat, stirring to dissolve the sugar. When you can't see sugar granules, turn down the heat and simmer for about 12 minutes, until the plums are juicy. Dump the plums and their juices into a blender or food processor and pulse into a chunky puree. Cool.

Whisk the egg whites with the remaining 2/3 cup sugar in a medium heatproof bowl. Place over a saucepan of simmering water (see page 218) and continue to whisk until thick and frothy, about 5 minutes. You may also do this in the bowl of a stand mixer to make the next step easier. *Just make sure the bottom does not touch the simmering water.*

Remove from the heat and transfer to the bowl of a stand mixer fitted with the whisk attachment. Beat on high speed until thick and glossy, about 5 minutes. Transfer to a clean bowl. Clean the mixer bowl and whisk attachment.

Whip the cream to soft peaks in a stand mixer fitted with the whisk attachment. Gently fold into the beaten whites until just combined. Gently swirl in the plum puree. *Don't overmix—we are going for a marbled effect.*

Pour into the loaf pan and cover with plastic wrap. Lightly drop the loaf pan on the counter to burst any large air bubbles trapped in the mixture.

Freeze until firm. *It'll take at least 8 hours.*

To dish up, unwrap the top layer of plastic and invert the loaf onto a serving platter. Remove the plastic wrap and cut into 8 slices. You may need to let the loaf soften for about 5 minutes before cutting. *Dip a knife in hot water before slicing for cleaner slices.* Serve immediately.

Leftover Scraps

Egg yolks—custard, scrambled, cake

Egg shells—clarifying stock, deacidifying coffee

Plum pits—flavor liquor

Overripe Banana SHEET CAKE
with Peanut Butter Frosting

Imagine that banana bread and birthday cake had a love child. Ultra-brown bananas deliver caramelized sweetness that is addictive. **SERVES 15** *It's rich!*

Cake

1 1/2 sticks (12 tablespoons) unsalted butter, plus more for the pan

4 brown bananas, peeled and chopped (about 3 cups)

3 cups all-purpose flour

2 1/2 teaspoons baking powder

1 1/4 teaspoons sea salt

3/4 teaspoon baking soda

4 large eggs, left out at room temp for about an hour

1 3/4 cups packed light brown sugar

2 cups buttermilk

1 (14-ounce) can sweetened condensed milk

1 (12-ounce) can evaporated milk

Peanut Butter Frosting

3 sticks (24 tablespoons) unsalted butter, softened at room temp

1 1/2 cups creamy peanut butter

1/4 cup honey

1 1/2 teaspoons fine sea salt

5 cups powdered sugar

Flaky sea salt, such as Maldon, for topping

Handful chopped roasted peanuts, for topping

To make the cake: Turn the oven to 350°F and line a standard 13 × 18-inch rimmed baking sheet with parchment paper. Coat the parchment with a thin film of butter. *Use the butter wrapper to hold the butter.*

Melt the butter in a large skillet over medium heat and cook for about 5 minutes, stirring when it looks like it needs it, until browned. Turn the heat down to low and add the bananas, mashing with a fork until they're practically smooth. Remove from the heat and pour into a large bowl to cool.

Mix the flour, baking powder, salt, and baking soda in another bowl.

Mix the eggs, brown sugar, and 1 cup of the buttermilk into the bananas until smooth. Stir in the dry ingredients. Pour and scrape the cake batter into the prepared pan and even out the surface. When the oven is up to temp, bake until browned and risen and a toothpick stuck into the center comes out clean, about 30 minutes. Put on a rack and cool for about 5 minutes.

Mix the remaining 1 cup buttermilk, the condensed milk, and the evaporated milk in a bowl. Poke holes on top of the warm cake with a skewer or long fork. Pour a quarter of the milk mixture slowly over the cake, letting it soak in before adding the rest in two more additions. Cool the cake to room temp.

To make the frosting: Beat the butter and peanut butter in a stand mixer fitted with the whisk attachment until fluffy, about 3 minutes. Beat in the honey and salt. Add the powdered sugar in three additions, scraping down the sides of the bowl a few times to keep everything evenly

blended and smooth. Beat for
a few more minutes, until very
fluffy.

Spread the frosting over
the top of the cooled cake.
Sprinkle with flaky salt and
peanuts. Cut into squares on
a 3-by-5 grid and serve.

Leftover Scraps

Egg shells—clarifying stock,
deacidifying coffee

Carrot Pulp LOAF CAKE WITH Brown Sugar Mascarpone

My grandma brings the carrot ring. Holidays would be incomplete without it. Hers is savory and comes to the table as a side dish, but I took it as inspiration for this sweet dessert version. **SERVES 8**

Cake

1 cup grapeseed oil, plus more for the pan

1 ¹/₄ cups all-purpose flour

1 ¹/₂ teaspoons baking powder

1 ¹/₂ teaspoons ground cinnamon

¹/₂ teaspoon fine sea salt

3 eggs, any size

1 cup packed light brown sugar

2 tablespoons grated fresh ginger *no need to peel*

1 ¹/₂ cups carrot pulp *Leftover from juicing. Your local juice shop may even give you pulp for free.* 💲

Brown Sugar Mascarpone

1 (13-ounce) container mascarpone cheese, softened at room temp

¹/₂ cup heavy cream

2 tablespoons light brown sugar

1 tablespoon fresh grated orange zest for garnish, if you want

To make the cake: Turn the oven to 350°F and lightly oil a 9 × 5-inch loaf pan. Line the bottom with parchment paper.

Mix the flour, baking powder, cinnamon, and salt in a small bowl.

Beat the eggs and brown sugar in a stand mixer fitted with the whisk attachment until light and fluffy, about 3 minutes. Slowly beat in the oil and ginger. Stir in the dry ingredients and carrot pulp until just combined. Pour into the prepared loaf pan.

When the oven is up to temp, bake until the top springs back when poked and a toothpick inserted in the crack in the top comes out with just a crumb or two clinging to it, about 45 minutes. Put the pan on a wire rack and cool for about 30 minutes. Run a knife around the edges, invert the pan, and remove the cake. Return the cake to the rack and cool all the way.

To make the topping: Beat the mascarpone, cream, and brown sugar in the bowl of a stand mixer fitted with the whisk attachment until light and fluffy, about 3 minutes. Slather onto the cake and sprinkle with the orange zest, if wanted.

Leftover Scraps

Egg shells—clarifying stock, deacidifying coffee

Zested orange—juice, fruit salads, cocktails, marinades, salad dressing

Bruised Pear PANDOWDY

Nothing bruises more easily than a ripe pear. So, when pears get stacked for sale, a lot of them inevitably get bumped and bruised. Even though they're unloved, I wanted to put them on a pear pandowdy pedestal! **SERVES 10**

Crust

1 ½ cups all-purpose flour, plus more for the board

1 tablespoon granulated sugar

½ teaspoon fine sea salt

1 stick (8 tablespoons) cold unsalted butter, cut into thin slices

⅓ cup plus 1 tablespoon cold buttermilk

Filling and assembly

1 cup granulated sugar, plus more for sprinkling on the crust

6 tablespoons unsalted butter, cut into small pieces

12 ripe or overripe Bartlett pears, cored, chopped rough

Finely grated zest and juice of 1 lemon

¼ cup all-purpose flour

3-finger pinch of fine sea salt

A little buttermilk for brushing on the crust

Vanilla ice cream, for serving

To make the crust: Mix the flour, sugar, and salt in a large bowl. Add the butter and pinch into small pieces with your fingertips until the pieces are the size of split peas. *Alternatively, freeze your butter and shred it on the large teeth of a box grater.*

Mix in the buttermilk using a fork to form a shaggy dough. Dump out onto a floured work surface and gently press into a rough blob. Flatten into a disk (this will make it easier to roll out later), wrap in plastic, and refrigerate for at least 1 hour. The pie dough can be refrigerated for several days before rolling it out to form a crust. *The dough may need 10 minutes at room temp before rolling out.*

When ready to bake, turn the oven to 400°F. Grease a 4-quart baking dish. *Use your butter wrappers.*

To make the filling: Moisten the sugar with 2 tablespoons water in a large skillet. Put over high heat and boil, swirling to help dissolve the sugar evenly, until the syrup becomes caramel colored, about 5 minutes. Turn the heat down to low and whisk in the butter. *At first the caramel will become lumpy and ugly, but just keep whisking, it'll smooth out.* Add the pears, lemon zest and juice, flour, and salt. Cook for about 10 minutes, stirring often, until the pears lose their raw look. Remove from the heat and pour into the prepared baking dish. Cool. *Add a shot (or two) of apple brandy or cognac to the simmering pears for a grown-up twist.*

Sprinkle a little flour on your work surface and roll out the

pastry to ¼-inch thickness. *No need to be precise in the shape of the crust. You will be tearing it into pieces.*

Cut or tear the dough into rough 2-inch pieces. Arrange the pieces over the pears, overlapping them slightly.

Brush with a little buttermilk and sprinkle with sugar.

When the oven is up to temp, bake until golden brown and bubbling, about 1 hour, turning the pan halfway through. Cool for 15 minutes, then serve with ice cream.

Leftover Scraps

Squeezed lemon—Preserved Squeezed Lemons (page 253), grilled lemon garnish

Pear cores—pear sauce, pear butter, flavor liquor

Spent Grain GRAHAM CRACKERS

I probably appreciate graham crackers *of any kind* more than the next person, but a homemade graham cracker has to be irresistible to anyone. In this version, I especially love what the spent grain flour brings. Its toasty, slightly malty, almost chocolaty richness makes it unique. Spent grain flour is just becoming a thing. Ask your local breweries if they've got any spent grain that you can grind, or order the flour online. **SERVES 8**

2 cups all-purpose flour

$1/2$ cup spent grain flour

1 cup packed dark brown sugar

1 teaspoon baking soda

$3/4$ teaspoon salt

1 $1/2$ teaspoons ground cinnamon

1 stick (8 tablespoons) cold unsalted butter, cut into chunks

$1/3$ cup pure maple syrup

$1/3$ cup milk, any type

3 tablespoons granulated sugar

Put the flours, brown sugar, baking soda, salt, and $1/2$ teaspoon of the cinnamon in a food processor. Pulse a few times to combine. Add the butter and pulse until the mixture looks like coarse sand. *You should still be able to see specks of butter.*

Pour in the maple syrup and milk and pulse a few times, until you get to a thick dough. *Scrape the bowl to help it along.*

Put a big piece of plastic wrap on the counter and dump the dough onto the plastic. Pat into a rectangle (about 1 inch thick), wrap in the plastic, and stick in the fridge for a couple of hours (or overnight).

When you're ready to bake, turn the oven to 350°F. Line two baking sheets with silicone baking mats or parchment paper.

Divide the dough in half. Flour one of the pieces on a work surface and roll out the dough into a pretty thin sheet (about $1/8$ inch thick) as close to a square as possible. Cut into squares. Slide onto one baking sheet. Do the same thing with the rest of the dough and the other baking sheet.

Mix together the sugar and the rest of the cinnamon and sprinkle over the crackers. Lightly poke the crackers all over with a fork. Throw in the freezer for about 10 minutes to firm up.

When the oven is up to temp, bake the crackers until browned but not too dark on the edges, about 20 minutes. The crackers will be a little soft but will firm up as they cool on racks, at least 20 minutes.

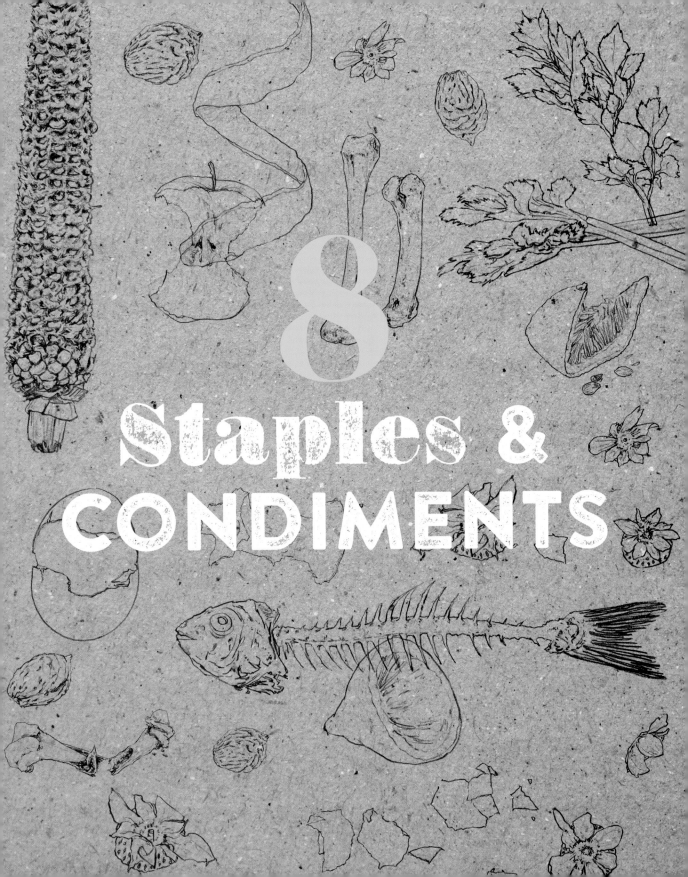

8
Staples &
CONDIMENTS

CHICKEN BACK STOCK (PAGE 244);
RENDERED FAT

Squeezed *lemons*

Apple CORES

Fish Bone STOCK

Your chowder, risotto, and cioppino are about to live at a whole 'nother level. **MAKES 2 QUARTS**

1 tablespoon vegetable oil

2 cups onion scraps  or 1 onion, chopped fine

1 cup celery trimmings or 2 ribs celery, chopped fine

5 pounds fish bones from any white-fleshed fish

3 cups white wine, not sweet

Coarsely grated zest and juice of 1 large lemon

Sea salt and fresh ground black pepper

2 sprigs fresh dill or 6 dill stems

2 sprigs fresh Italian (flat-leaf) parsley or 6 parsley stems

Add the oil to a large saucepan or Dutch oven and put over medium heat. Add the onion and celery and stir to coat with oil. Cover and cook for 10 minutes, or until the veggies are aromatic. Add the fish bones, cover, and cook until they lose their raw look, about 5 more minutes.

Add the wine, raise the heat to medium-high, and boil for 5 minutes. Add the lemon zest, lemon juice, a little S&P, dill, parsley, and enough water to cover. When the stock boils, turn down the heat and skim away any scum that has risen to surface. Simmer for 40 minutes. Strain and refrigerate for up to 2 days, or freeze for up to 3 months.

Leftover Scraps

Squeezed lemon—Preserved Squeezed Lemons (page 253), grilled lemon garnish

Chicken Back
STOCK

Homemade chicken stock is great. Using backs for your bones makes it impeccable. **MAKES ABOUT 2 GALLONS**

5 pounds uncooked chicken bones and/or parts (backs, necks, gizzards, hearts, and trimmings) 💲

1 cup carrot trimmings and peelings 💲 or 2 carrots, chopped

1 cup celery trimmings 💲 or 2 ribs celery, chopped

2 cups onion scraps 💲 or 1 onion, chopped

2 teaspoons sea salt

1 tablespoon whole black peppercorns

2 teaspoons dried thyme or 2 tablespoons fresh thyme

1 whole clove

1 bay leaf

10 stems Italian (flat-leaf) parsley 💲

Put the chicken in a large soup pot, cover with water, and bring to a boil over high heat. Turn down the heat and skim away any scum that has risen to surface. Add the carrot, celery, onion, salt, peppercorns, thyme, clove, bay leaf, and parsley. Simmer for 3 hours, strain out the solids, and let cool. Refrigerate for up to 5 days, or freeze for up to 3 months. Use for soups, sauces, and stews.

Veg Scraps STOCK

This book is chocked with ways to take advantage of veg scraps. None of them are more universal than stock. **MAKES ABOUT 1 GALLON**

2 tablespoons vegetable oil

5 pounds vegetable scraps and trimmings, such as onions, leeks, celery, fennel, carrots, parsnips, mushrooms, tomatoes, and garlic 💲

1 bay leaf

12 whole black peppercorns

2 teaspoons dried thyme or 2 tablespoons fresh thyme

1 tablespoon coarse sea salt

1 teaspoon ground turmeric

2 whole cloves

⅓ cup chopped parsley stems 💲

Put a large soup pot over medium heat. Add the oil, wait a beat, and add the vegetables. Cook until the vegetables soften, stirring every now and then. Add the bay leaf, peppercorns, thyme, salt, turmeric, cloves, and parsley and cover with water by 2 inches or so. When it boils, skim away any scum that rises to the surface. Reduce the heat and simmer for 2 hours, then strain and let cool. Refrigerate for up to 3 days, or freeze for up to 6 months.

Herb Stem SALT

The aromatic juices in herb stems are the power ingredients in this flavored salt. **MAKES ¹/₂ CUP**

3 tablespoons finely chopped green herb stems, such as mint, parsley, basil, sage, and/or tarragon

5 tablespoons coarse sea salt, preferably grey salt (sel gris)

Crush the herb stems in a mortar and pestle until they are all busted up and juicy. Add the salt, 2 tablespoons at a time, and crush into the herbs until ground fine. *It's OK if there are some medium-size salt grains.*

Put in a tightly closed container and use within 2 weeks.

Yesterday's **Breadcrumbs**

Seems pretty obvious that homemade breadcrumbs kick store-bought's butt. **MAKES 2 CUPS FRESH OR 1 1/2 CUPS TOASTED**

4 ounces hard stale bread
1/2 teaspoon olive oil (for toasted breadcrumbs)

Shred the bread with the large teeth of a box grater, or cut into small cubes and chop fine in a food processor. Use right away or store in the freezer for up to 2 months.

For toasted breadcrumbs, turn the oven to 350°F.

Work the breadcrumbs with the oil on a rimmed baking sheet using your hands to distribute the oil as much as you can. *It's OK if it's not completely evenly dispersed.* Bake until browned and crisp, about 6 minutes, stirring once halfway through. Use right away, or store in a tightly closed container in a dark cabinet for up to 1 month.

Apple Core BUTTER

Just because you stop eating before you get to the core doesn't mean you're done. There's lots more love left. **MAKES ABOUT 1 CUP**

12 large apple cores (about 1 pound), chopped small

½ cup granulated sugar

1 teaspoon ground cinnamon

2-finger pinch of ground allspice

2-finger pinch of salt

Small pinch of ground cloves

Small grating of nutmeg

Mix everything in a medium heavy-bottomed saucepan and cook over low heat until the bottom of the pot looks a little wet, about 2 minutes, stirring all the time. Cover the pot and cook until the apple cores are absolutely soft, stirring and mashing with a wooden spoon every now and then. Do not try to speed this up. You'll burn the mix. If the mixture gets so dry that it starts to stick, add a tablespoon or so of water. Keep cooking and mashing until the mixture is very thick and aromatic, about 20 minutes.

Cool for 10 minutes. Puree with a stick blender or in a food processor. Push through a strainer using a rubber spatula to remove any bits that didnt get pureed. Store in a tightly closed container in the refrigerator for up to 1 month. Use in Bacon Fat Biscuit and Apple Butter Sandwiches (page 36) or Apple Core Butter Roasted Duck (page 171).

Whole Lemon CURD

This is no la-di-da lemon curd. It's got moxie. It's too bitter, too sweet, too rustic, and too dang delicious. **MAKES 2 CUPS**

2 lemons, halved and chopped coarse

1/2 vanilla bean

2 cups granulated sugar

3 eggs, any size

1/4 teaspoon coarse sea salt

1/2 stick (4 tablespoons) butter

Put a pot of water over medium heat and bring to a boil.

Meanwhile, combine the lemons, vanilla, sugar, eggs, and salt in a blender and blend until smooth. *A few chunks of lemon won't matter.* Pour into a bowl that fits nicely onto the pot of water. With the water boiling, cook the curd, stirring every now and then, until the mixture is lightly thickened, the consistency of pancake batter. Remove the bowl from the pot and whisk the butter into the warm curd.

Strain into a storage container, cover, and refrigerate. Use within 3 months.

PRESERVED Squeezed Lemons

Preserved lemons are exotic and expensive. You can turn all of your squeezed lemon halves into this luxury ingredient for no money at all. **MAKES 1 PINT**

3/4 cup coarse sea salt

10 spent (juiced) lemon halves

2 tablespoons cracked coriander seeds

Put 2 tablespoons of the salt in a pint jar. Put 1 tablespoon salt in the squeezed-out shell of each lemon half and pack it into the jar, one at a time. Top with the coriander seeds and enough hot water to completely cover the lemons. Seal the jar and set on a table to cure for about 3 days, turning and shaking the jar as much as you want, *but at least once a day*. Put in the refrigerator and let it hang out until the lemons are softened and meaty, about 3 weeks. Use anytime over the next year.

Grapefruit Rind MARMALADE

At first taste, grapefruit rinds are inedible—pithy, spongy, and bitter. Just add sugar and you've got marmalade. *Good save!* **MAKES 2 CUPS**

Rind from 2 grapefruits
1 ½ cups granulated sugar
½ cup water
¼ teaspoon salt

Simmer everything in a heavy saucepan over super-low heat until the peel is completely soft and syrupy, about 3 hours. Add a tablespoon more water every now and then to keep the marmalade moist. Mush in a food processor. It keeps in the refrigerator for up to 6 months.

Scrappy Water

This is the easiest win in the book. When you have no clue about what to do with your fruit scraps, soak them in water and turn the mundane into the extraordinary. **MAKES 1 QUART**

2 cups overripe bruised fruit (if large, cut into 1/4-inch pieces) and/or cucumbers or celery, cut into 1/4-inch pieces

1/4 cup chopped fresh herbs, your choice

1 quart cold spring or filtered water

In a pitcher, combine the fruits and/or vegetables and herbs with the cold water and wait at least 10 minutes to develop the flavor. Chill overnight for the fullest flavor. It will have enough flavor, but not a lot, in as little as 5 minutes.

RENDERED Animal Fat

Replace oil and butter with rendered fat and your cooking game will explode. All of the following recipes use pretty much the same cooking method. **MAKES 8 OUNCES**

Chicken or Duck (Schmaltz)

1 pound raw chicken or duck fat, no bits of skin, bone, meat, or juices

Beef or Lamb (Tallow)

1 pound raw trimmed beef or lamb fat, no meat or blood spots *Suet is the best.*

Pork (Lard)

1 pound raw trimmed pork belly or fatback, no meat, skin, or blood spots

2 big pinches of coarse sea salt

Put the fat in the freezer until it is firm, about 30 minutes. Cut it into small chunks and freeze again to firm it back up, about 10 minutes. Chop in a food processor until it is in really small pieces, sort of the size of ground beef.

Put the fat and salt in a heavy saucepan over very low heat. Simmer until the fat is liquid and the cracklings are browned, stirring when you think it needs it, about 30 minutes for schmaltz, 3 to 4 hours for tallow, and 2 to 3 hours for lard.

Pick out the big solid pieces of crackling and have a snack. Pour the liquid fat and the little dusty pieces of crackling through a gold coffee filter or a strainer lined with cheesecloth and store the clear liquid fat in a tightly closed container in the refrigerator for up to 3 months.

ACKNOWLEDGMENTS

Before I start thanking everyone who made this book possible, I want to acknowledge my amazing wife, Angiolina. Ang, I cannot imagine navigating life without you. Everything I am is made that much better by our love for one another. As you well know, I am all over the place most of the time. No one brings me back to earth and centers me more than you do. You are the foundation on which all of the rest is built.

Food is sticky. It brings people together, and I found early on the magic of making and sharing food with the people I love. So, the first people I want to thank are the first people I cooked for, my whole loud, crazy, amazing family, Shauna, Alex, Erin, Nanny, Papa, Grandma Judith and Grandpa Hillel, for seeing the value of what I do and cheering me on.

My love of cooking has tested most of my friendships. I want to recognize a bunch of people here for forcing down my experimental meals and for telling me the truth. You are the guys who spit out the bad and let me know when I nailed it. First, the Jew crew: Jordan, Feldy, Trem, Dave, and Ruby. You were my first buddies. We learned to make the best out of what was in the fridge, and I now know that was the beginning of cooking scrappy. Then there's the UConn boys: Deano, Snoop, Bobby, and Ribchin. You came to my first dinner parties and together we figured out how to MacGyver the crap out of food—from mixing dough in helmets, to mastering the art of cooking on a hot plate. I can't believe how much hanging out with you gave me. Then there's the folks from cooking school, mostly my buddies Ben Witten, Sarah Coles, and Shiyam Sundar. You were the first people I met who loved food just as much as I did. You let me know that I wasn't alone. We were of the same breed and you will always be my family.

Six years into working in professional kitchens, I was worn out, depressed, and lost. Thank God I found Sur La Table, and my calling—to motivate other people to jump in the kitchen with me. My Sur La Table family has always had my back. They believed in me when I was still having doubts and they have been incredibly generous, offering me fulfilling professional opportunities that hit so many of our mutual goals. Thank you, Ed, Jack, Ben, Jeff, Mary, Tracy, Doralece, Shira, Urbano, Pete, Billy, Jacob, Robb, Natalie, Nathan, Elizabeth, and all the teams at HQ and the teams in the field.

Through SLT, I was introduced to Nikki Lockett and Carly Smith, and the whole Kitchen Aid team. Thanks for "mixing up" the food waste revolution with me. I could not imagine better partners in crime.

Sur La Table sent me to NYC in 2011. I did not want to go. But in the back of my mind I knew it was the best place to be if I was serious about inspiring people to cook. Shira Zackai held my hand and led me into the world of New York media, introducing me to the *Today Show*, *Good Morning America*, and the show that changed my professional life, *Katie*, where I met and became friends with Katie Couric. Katie—Without your mentorship and belief in me there is no chance I would be here today. You are a walking inspiration.

Katie opened many doors and opportunities for me, and the most important one was the production of my own show, Scraps, where I met one of my closest friends and *Scraps* show-runner, Tim Whitney. Our show, our baby, is as much Tim's as it is mine. His dedication, loyalty, and talent continue to inspire me on a daily basis. There is no one I would trust more in the trenches or have more fun with riding the roller coaster of life. Then there's Clare Langan, the culinary producer of *Scraps*, who brings all my ridiculous ideas into reality. You are one awesome chef! And of course, thank you to the entire production crew of *Scraps*, who bring the essential message of ending food waste into people's homes in a way that inspires them to make the world a better place to live.

Mark Bitterman was the guest on the Port-land, Oregon, episode of the first season of *Scraps*. Mark showed me that I needed to write a book, and he introduced me to Andy Schloss, my word Yoda, and the coauthor of this book. Thank you, Andy, for finding my voice and amplifying it louder and clearer than it ever was. You are truly one of the greater talents I have met.

To Jim Henkens, the amazing photographer for *Cooking Scrappy*: This book leaps off the page because of your stunning photos, thoughtful approach, and honest eye. And much thanks to Callie Meyer, who styled the food and props, for her incredibly hard work and uncompromising will to make even the scrappiest food look sexy.

Thank you to my agent, Janis Donnaud, for introducing me to the extraordinary team at Harper Wave. I adore the book they crafted! It is more beautiful, smarter, and more alive than I ever could have imagined. They made my first step into publishing unbelievably gratifying. I am indebted to you, Karen Rinaldi. I have never met anyone more outrageously passionate for what they do. To Hannah Robinson: You're a total rock star. Thanks for bringing spunk and energy to every page of *Cooking Scrappy*. And to Leah Carlson-Stanisic, our designer: My dream for this book was to turn forgotten ingredients into incredible food. Your design has magnified that dream, making a book of scraps into a work of art.

And a special thank you to everyone who stands for the bruised, the forgotten, and the back of the fridge. I am proud to stand with you!

Love, Joel

INDEX

eggs *(continued)*

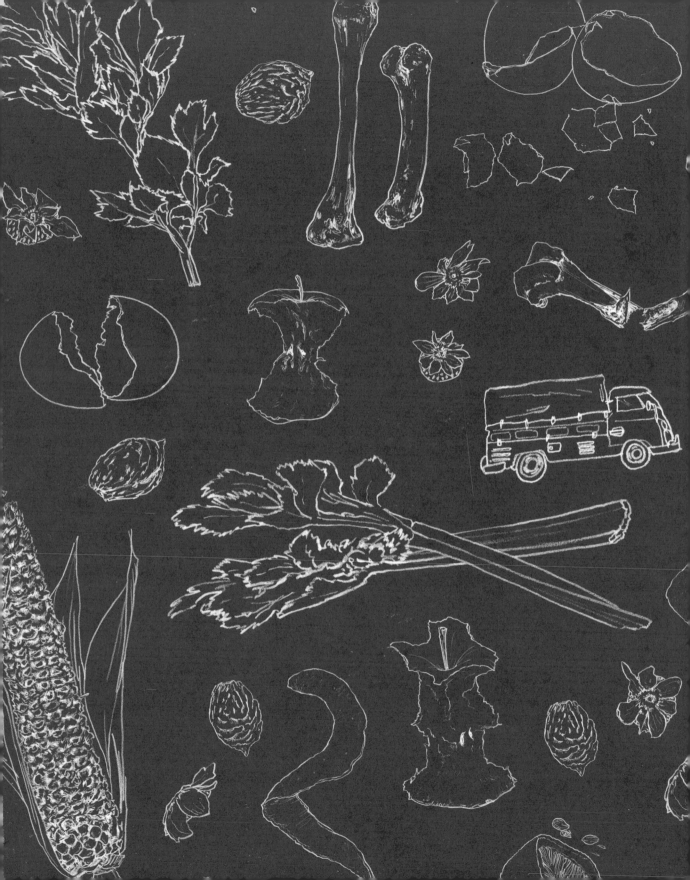